Wisdom of the Quran

Mhamed Aboulalaa

ISBN: 9781520592343

Contents

Contents

ii

Contents

Introduction

The Quran is an exceptional book. It is the holy book of Islam, and most importantly, is considered as the literal words (verbatim) of God and not a human inspired text. It was revealed to the Prophet Muhammad fourteen centuries ago as a message of God to all mankind and not to a specific community.

The purpose of this book is, first to present concisely, and hopefully clearly, the main lines of this message and parts of the wisdom contained in the Quran, and second to provide an introduction that helps for an exhaustive reading of the Text.

The Quran is a very special text in its structure, style and content. The order of its arrangement follows considerations that may appear after careful examination of the Text; they are not chronological, nor thematic. Its style is characterised by alternation of narrative passages, exhortations, messages of guidance, hope, warnings, etc. with variations in the rhythms depending on the chapters (called Surah).

Its content encompasses a wide range of subjects: information about God, arguments about His existence and Unity, the Creation, the evidences (called signs) for all that, moral values, prescription about the relationship of Man to God, parents, family and the others, messages about human destiny such as the hereafter, life after death; the later information being beyond human knowledge, only the Creator can provide it through His revelation. These subjects are also linked to the questions of the purpose of life, of man's existence, to which the Quran provides clarifications and answers.

On the other hand anyone of us, regardless of his convictions, would ask himself existential questions like: who we are, what is the purpose of our creation and of the creation of the universe, which rules of conduct should we adopt in our life, what would happen after death etc.

Furthermore once we are led to the idea of the existence of a God, the Creator of the universe, we naturally expect from Him to provide us indications on these deep questions, considering that only God can give us the truth on subjects about which Man can only speculate.

The Quran is precisely devoted to give answers to these questions whatever may be our origins, our background, our level of instruction, our age and experience, our maturity, our time, be it the seventh or the twenty first century. A book that meets these requirements and many others in addition to providing more information (see below) would certainly be highly specific in every aspect.

Although significant parts of the Quran can be understood easily at a first reading, other parts require explanations and sometimes elaborate interpretations or exegesis contrary to other usual literal texts. This book tries to give a direct access to the message of the Quran throughout main topics like:

- The basic principle of Islam, the Unity of God which is the belief in a unique God, the Creator and Sustainer of the universe and the related consequences.
- The emphasis of the Quran on learning and constant quest of knowledge which is essential in developing Man's thinking capabilities and reason, instruments considered as fundamental in Man's life.
- Worship prescriptions concerning the relation of Man to God.
- Moral values which turn out to be similar to the widely adopted values in modern societies.

- Work and good deeds, urging Man to do his best in this regard, and this is a basic criterion of the assessment of humans for their rewards.
- Charity, spending for the needy understood in a broad sense and considered as an instrument for social solidarity and symbolizing the love of the other and also preventing blind attachment to money and other material goods which one would necessarily leave behind him.
- Tolerance at individual, collective and religious levels.

Each of these subjects may lead to elaborate discussions, but the presentation made in this book is kept concise although we try to highlight some deep ideas and subtleties that appear when analysing some topics.

With its content, the Quran presents itself as a book of guidance that aims to insure the successfulness of man in his life and in the hereafter:

"There has come to you from God a (new) light and a perspicuous Book, -Where with God guides all who seek His good pleasure to ways of peace and safety" The Table 5:15-16

At the collective side, the Quran points out that the human diversity comes intentionally from God's will, and consequently advocates tolerance and open-mindedness for peaceful coexistence between nations and communities :

"O mankind! We created you from a male and a female, and made you into nations and tribes, that you may know each other. Verily the most honoured of you in the sight of God is the most righteous of you. And God is All-Knowing, All-Aware". The Apartments 49:13

As it will be seen, Islam through its fundamental Text, the Quran (along with the Prophet Muhammed tradition) is, in fact, a message of wisdom, tolerance and moral improvement for humankind, to all the people.

M. A.

February 2017

Remark. There is already an extensive literature on the Quran and Islam which is available in many languages other than Arabic. Besides the translations of the Quran, many highly valuable works (printed or online) exist. There are also extensive resources in particular online that try to present the Quran and Islam; but sometimes this is done either partially or by emphasizing many secondary issues and even providing distorted ideas for various reasons. On the other hand Islam is subject to numerous stereotypes and prejudices that find a breeding ground in contexts of violence phenomena mixed with religious considerations. Therefore, works and materials that provide accurate information about this religion along with a better communication are constantly needed and welcomed. We hope that this work although not exhaustive would contribute to satisfying this need.

Considerations on the English translation used

The translation adopted in this book is that of A.Yusuf Ali. Slight modifications have been made in order to simplify the wording with more direct sentences, to clarify the meaning or to substitute more modern English expressions or to give another English counterpart of few important concepts (see below). When seeking the most appropriate rendering we were helped by many other valuable translations among them those of:

Muhammad M. Pickthall, The Meaning of the Glorious Quran (1930).
Arthur Arberry, The Koran Interpreted (1955).
Thomas B. Irving, The Noble Quran (1992).
Muhammad Asad, The Message of the Quran (1980)
Muhammad M. Khan and Muhammad T. Al-Hilali, Interpretation of the Meanings of the Noble Quran (1977, 1999).
M.A.S. Abdel-Haleem, The Qur'an (2004).
Maulana Wahiduddin Khan, The Quran (2009).
Talal Itani, Quran in Clear English (2012).

The reader may find elsewhere comments and assessments about the English translations of the Quran.
We point out here that many of the numerous translations contain inaccuracies, mistranslations and mistakes and are not free from biases either religious, sectarians or political.

Let us also mention one of the many difficulties in a work of translation of the Quran : the difficult choice between on one hand a literal translation which would intend to be faithful to the original Arabic Quran but would not provide clear meaning of many parts that require specific background and on the other hand an explanatory translation which translates each verse by its meaning or what is believed to be, in which case the translator is supposed to have an unequivocal interpretation of each part.

Each verse of the Quran has obviously to be understood before being translated. While this understanding is clear in most part of the Text, it is not so for other parts, and one has to make appeal to interpretations, exegesis or a proper understanding and sometimes points of view which can be either objective and neutral or oriented by specific biases as mentioned before.

Besides the important works of Marmaduk Pictthal, Muhammad Asad and Thomas Irving, the relative recent works of Abdel-Halim, Maulana Wahiduddin Khan, and Itani seem to have reached a good stage of accuracy, seeking expressions which stick as much as possible to the original Text and providing an understandable meaning, while keeping concise the rendering as it is in the Arabic Quran.

However, it should be brought to attention that it is hard to claim the reach of a perfect counterpart of the Quran in English or any other language and there is a widespread view that the Quran cannot be translated but only interpreted, in particular because any translation cannot reproduce the linguistic, stylistic and even emotional attributes of the original Arabic. The work of Arthur J.Arberry, which seems to be one of the best of non-Muslim translations, was, according to the author, precisely motivated by this challenge to reproduce these formal characteristics of the Quran; in his introduction he mentioned:

"In choosing to call the present work *The Koran Interpreted* I have conceded the relevancy of the orthodox Muslim view, of which Pickthall, for one, was so conscious, that the Koran is untranslatable. Some of the implications of that doctrine are sketched out in the preface to my *The Holy Koran: an Introduction with Selections* (Allen & Unwin,1955), and it is not proposed to repeat the same argument here. Briefly, the rhetoric and rhythm of the Arabic of the Koran are so characteristic, so powerful, so highly emotive, that any version whatsoever is bound in the nature of things to be but a poor copy of the glittering splendour of the original. Never was it more true than in this instance that *traduttore traditore*. My chief reason for offering this new version of a book which has been 'translated' many times already is that in no previous rendering has a serious attempt been made to imitate, however imperfectly, those rhetorical and rhythmical patterns which are the glory and the sublimity of the Koran. I am breaking new ground here; it may therefore be thought appropriate to explain in short my intentions and my method ..."

Notes on the translations of some important terms of the Quran

There are few terms used in the Quran which give rise to important concepts that go far beyond their initial meaning in Arabic. The translation in these cases has therefore to be considered carefully, for the use of some counterparts in English or any other language – which come quickly to mind – may lead to inaccuracies and deformations of the messages conveyed by the Quran.

The term Taqwa :

With its derivatives 'Ittaqa' (verb), "Al Mouttaqoun" (adjective, name) : This is the most important of the terms we referred to, that gives rise to a cardinal concept explained in detail in the chapter "Selected topics" of this book.

The literal meaning of the quality "Taqwa" is related to "the protection of oneself towards something feared" and in the context of the Quran it is used in the sense of taking care in being righteous, doing good deeds, avoiding evil and manifestly bad actions that could lead to a displeasure of God.

7

This is an example of terms that the Quran uses in a sense much specific than its literal meaning and furthermore the careful reader of the Quran will notice that precise attributes, characteristic to this quality of Taqwa are given by the Quran itself

Many English translations use the terms "fearing God" or "God-fearing" (for the name of those who have this quality). We see that this is not completely accurate: unless explanations are provided in order to show what this means in the context of the Quran, the reader of such a rendering may be misled. In fact the concept of "Taqwa" with its meaning and consequences form a whole chapter of the Islamic studies.

This has led some translators to use other counterparts like: God-consciousness (Muhammad Asad) and God-mindfulness (Abdel-Halim, Maulana Khan).

However in some places, the expression "God-fearing" can reflect faithfully the meaning. So in the present book, we shall use expressions derived from "God-mindfulness", and also keep those derived from "God-fearing" (used in the Yusuf Ali's translation adopted here) when this is possible.

The term "Kafir" :

With the related words such as "Kafara" (the verb) and "Al Kufr" (the name of the quality): this is also a very delicate concept which deserves a very cautious translation because those who may have the attributes summarized by the adjective "Kafir" in the Quran are those who would face the displeasure of God and His disapproval, at the very opposite of the righteous.

English and other languages translations use in general the terms "unbeliever" or "disbeliever". This rendering is not accurate and may even be regrettable.

The use of inadequate translations may lead to consider that:

"Kafir" as an absolute adjective which when translated by unbeliever or disbeliever is the opposite of "believer" and probably the opposite of "Muslim" which leads to the false conclusion that one is either a believer or a "Kafir"; and since those who deserve the "Kafir" attribute are severely rebuked in the Quran, the consequences of such an inaccurate translation include negative impact on the reader and are among the sources of misunderstandings and prejudices about Islam.

At this stage let us point out that the same misunderstanding of this concept is valid within Muslims themselves and even within Muslim scholars.

The correct rendering of this concept is crucial especially with regards to the relationship between Muslims and non-Muslims and when one is concerned by the explanation of the authentic message of the Quran and Islam.

Let us briefly comment on this: In its literal meaning the verb "Kafara" means to conceal something; in the context of the Quran this is used for: concealing the truth, or the evidences which lead to the truth. In practice, this means to deny the truth or the evidences provided even if these are objectively clear.

Examples: The case of Moses: when he provides signs or evidences to Pharaoh that he is a Prophet from God, Pharaoh refused to accept this:

The Ant: 27:14
"But when Our Signs came to them, that should have opened their eyes, they said: 'This is sorcery manifest! '
And they rejected those Signs in iniquity and arrogance, though their souls were convinced thereof"

The case of Jesus:
The Table 5:110
"when you show them the clear Signs, and those who deny

9

[alladina Kafarou] among them said: 'This is nothing but evident magic.'"

So in many cases the verb "Kafara" refers to a situation of denial of evidences or truth by a person despite their objectivity and furthermore this person may be convinced by the facts presented but he still holds his initial position in denying the facts, the evidences, the truth, etc., because of pride and arrogance for instance.

Hence these words "Kafara", "Kafir", and "Kufr" are a second major example after the terms related to "Taqwa" which have a literal meaning (not necessarily well-known to many), and that the Quran uses for a specific meaning (or meanings, depending on the context) which deserve a careful study before choosing the most appropriate counterpart in any language.

Using words derived from the verb 'deny' seems to give a good solution in this case: when the terms related to 'Kafara' are used in the Quran with reference to a specific fact, the translation would be "to deny the thing or the fact (specified)" and when they refer to the general concept of "Kufr" the translation would be derived from the expression "to deny the Truth" : this rendering is adopted in the translation of Maulana Wahiduddin Khan.

We can also use simple expressions derived from the verb "to deny" without adding "the Truth" as is the case when M. Khan uses the expression "Those who deny the Truth".
It would be better if one could use the term "denier" meaning "the one who denies". That is the solution used by J.Bercque in his French translation: a new term "dénégateur" in French is preferred and chosen by this author who pointed out that current rendering like "infidèle" or "mécréant" ('non-faithful' which may be close to unbeliever) are not appropriate.

Part I :
The message of the Quran throughout some main topics

1 The spiritual side

1. Introduction

Introducing the Quran throughout its main topics is the method adopted in the present work to provide effectively a good insight into the sacred Text of Islam.

The Quran is the book of Islam, the last monotheist religion which was revealed to the Prophet Muhammed.

Islam has come after the monotheist religions, Christianity and Judaism and consists of the belief in a unique God, the Creator and Master of the universe, and the submission to His will.

Let us point out from the beginning a basic fact which is not well emphasized in the literature and that seems not to be a part of the ideas that many have about Islam : the belief first in God, His existence, and second that Muhammed is His Prophet and Messenger, is demanded to men not as a pure dogma to be accepted without reflection and internal conviction ; on the contrary, in the argumentations of the Quran, one will find on one hand elements that dismiss some ancient believes of men presented as naively acquired, without reflection and careful examination and on the other hand many elements and arguments urging men to make use of reason and reflection in order to establish strong foundations for their convictions and believes (see §3.1).

Etymologically, the term Islam is linked to several other terms deriving from the root s.l.m which are related to concepts like: obedience, submission (to God), peace or salvation (Salute) (Salam), innocence (Salim), etc. Islam refers to a submission to God's will, obedience, devotion to Him. A Muslim is the one who observes this obedience.

An important fact is that at the religious level, the Quran considers that Islam according to the previous meaning (submission to God ('s will)) is the religion proclaimed and announced by all the Prophets. This begun with Noah who said:

Jonah 72:
"*I have been commanded to be of those who submit to God's will.*"

Then Abraham:

The Pilgrimage, 22:78
"*He has chosen you, and has imposed no difficulties on you in religion; it is the cult of your father Abraham. It is He Who has named you Muslims (those who submit to God's will), both before and in this (Revelation).*"

Then Moses:
Jonah 10:84
"*Moses said: 'O my people! If you do (really) believe in God, then in Him put your trust if you submit (your will to His').*"

And Jesus Christ:
The Family of Imran, 3:52
"*When Jesus found Unbelief on their part He said: 'Who will be My helpers to (the work of) God?' The disciples said: 'We are God's helpers: We believe in God, and bear witness that we are Submitted to God's will (Muslims in Arabic)'*".

2. The Quran and Islam confirm and complete the previous monotheist religions

There are many references on this point in the Quran, like :

The Family of Imran 3:1-3
"God! There is no god but He,-the Living, the Self-Subsisting, Eternal.
It is He Who sent down to you, in truth, the Book, confirming what went before it; and He sent down the Torah [Law of Moses] and the Gospel [of Jesus] before this, as a guide to mankind, and He sent down the criterion [of judgement between right and wrong]."

Islam has come with a set of principles and values with the intent to provide guidance to every human in his life. These are about:

a) Answers and thoughts about the fundamental existence questions: God (the Creator), the purpose of life, death, what will come after death, resurrection, the hereafter (which existence is an integral part of Islam's message as it was in the Jewish and Christian messages), etc.

b) Some prescriptions:
– the belief in God, the Creator of universe, which must follow from reason and reflection (thought), the only ways which allow to gain a true conviction as well as from the intuition and good sense;
– the prayer, the charity and spending for the needy, the fasting (in the month of Ramadan), and the pilgrimage to Mecca (for those who can afford it).

c) A set of moral values which address all aspects of life: from the quest of learning to individual behaviour, man's relationship with other people, including for instance the moral of work, rules regarding family issues, and moral values at individual and collective levels such as justice, tolerance, etc. The Quran talks about this purpose at its beginning:

The Cow 2:1-5
" *A.L.M. This is the Book in which there is no doubt, a guidance for those who are mindful of God;*
Who believe in the Unseen, are steadfast in prayer, and spend out of what We have provided for them;
And who believe in the Revelation sent to you, and sent before your time, and are certain of the Hereafter.
They are on true guidance from their Lord, and these will be the successful."

In the following, we shall outline succinctly these aspects.

3. The belief in God

It is the belief in God, His uniqueness, as The Creator and Master of the universe and of all the things existing in it. The Quran stresses the fact that this belief must follow from a strong conviction that can be acquired either by reason and reflection or by one's own internal intuition.

So, besides one's own feelings and intuition, when thinking about one's existence, destiny, the topics of life, death, which generally lead to the idea of the existence of one God, the Creator and master of the destiny of everything, the Quran calls on everybody to meditate on the evidences that establish this fact (proofs called sometimes signs), among them :

- The creation of humans and universe: the complexity, the order and the perfection of this creation cannot be a result of the chance. The Quran calls insistently on men to reflect on this fact which gives an obvious demonstration of the existence of a Creator.

Asserting the opposite idea would mean to hold, for instance, the view that matter elements have been assembled and arranged all by themselves (by some mysterious process) to form an infinitely complex body such as that of human beings with all its organs; for instance : the brain, the eyes, the ears, the mouth, the tongue, the heart, the lung, the liver, etc. Each of them has a distinct role and has a high degree of complexity, which are apprehended only very partially by the modern science.

– If one looks carefully on the constitution and functioning of only one organ such as the heart (not to mention the brain, the liver etc.), he would realize that every part of the body is carefully designed and planned to play a definite role in the life of the human body with interactions with other parts; is it possible that the heart for instance would have been designed and formed by a coincidence?

Is it possible that a computer, a car or just a house (with the doors, the windows, the curtains, the floors, the locks, etc.) could be constructed by chance, or by a sort of an evolution even within billions of years?

Can one believe that his house, with its furniture (Armchairs, beds, carpets, bookshelf, TV, kitchen appliances, etc.) could be built by chance even over millions of years?

The Quran refers to these facts in some verses like:

The Fig 95:4
"We created man in the best design."

The Ants 27:88

"And you see the mountains, and imagine them fixed, yet they pass, as the passing of the clouds—the making of God, who has perfected everything. He is fully Informed of what you do."

As the Quran is a book for all times, for all men whatever may be their stage of knowledge about nature and whatever may be their age, origin, culture, intellectual level, it provides argumentations that address all these audiences: on one hand by drawing attention to evidences from current observations and reasoning accessible to everyone and on the other hand making allusions to much more evolved facts which were subject to recent scientific progress, and forthcoming progress will certainly show other similar facts (see, e.g., the book of Dr. Maurice Bucaille):

The Pilgrimage 22: 5-7

"5.O mankind! if you have a doubt about the Resurrection, (consider) that We created you out of dust, then from a small drop, then out of a leech-like clot, then out of a morsel of flesh, partly formed and partly unformed, so that We may make (it) clear for you ; and We cause whom We will to rest in the wombs for an appointed term, then do We bring you out as babes, then (foster you) that you may reach your age of full strength; and some of you are called to die, and some are sent back to the feeblest old age, so that they know nothing after having known (much), and (further). And you see the earth barren and lifeless, but when We pour down rain on it, it is stirred (to life), it swells, and it puts forth every kind of beautiful growth (in pairs)"

"6.This is so, because God is the Reality: it is He Who gives life to the dead, and it is He Who has power over all things."
"7.And verily the Hour will come: there can be no doubt about it, or about (the fact) that God will raise up all who are in the graves."

- In addition to human being creation, the Quran draws attention to other signs which should incite man to reflect upon the Creation and His Creator:

The Family of Imran 3:190-191

"190 Behold! in the creation of the heavens and the earth, and the alternation of night and day,- there are indeed Signs for people of understanding,"-
"191 Those who celebrate the praises of God, standing, sitting, and lying down on their sides, and contemplate the (wonders of) creation in the heavens and the earth, With the thought : 'Our Lord! You did not create this in vain, Glory to You ! Preserve us from the doom of Fire.'"

The Romans 30:19-27

"30:19 It is He Who brings out the living from the dead, and brings out the dead from the living, and Who gives life to the earth after it is dead: and thus shall you be brought out (from the dead)."

"30:20 Among His Signs in this, that He created you from dust; and then,- behold, you are men scattered far and wide !"

"30:21 And among His Signs is this, that He created for you mates from among yourselves, that you may dwell in tranquillity with them, and He has put love and mercy between your : verily in that are Signs for people who reflect."

"30:22 And among His Signs is the creation of the heavens and the earth, and the variations in your languages and your colours: verily in that are Signs for those who know."

"30:23 And among His Signs is the sleep that you take by night and by day, and the quest that you make for (livelihood) out of His Bounty: verily in that are signs for people who listen."

"30:24 And among His Signs, He shows you the lightning, for a fear and a hope, and He sends down rain from the sky and with it

gives life to the earth after it is dead: verily in that are Signs for people who understand."

"30:25 And among His Signs is this, that heaven and earth stand by His Command: then when He calls you, by a single call, from the earth, behold, you come forth."

"30:26 To Him belongs every being that is in the heavens and on earth: all are devoutly obedient to Him."

"30:27 It is He Who begins the process of creation; then repeats it; and for Him it is most easy. To Him belongs the loftiest similitude in the heavens and the earth; for He is Exalted in Might, full of wisdom."

Furthermore, the Quran provides indications about God, with His attributes, for example in the Throne verse:

The Cow 2:255
"God! There is no god but He,-the Living, the Self-subsisting, The Sustainer. No slumber can seize Him nor sleep. His are all things in the heavens and on earth. Who is there can intercede in His presence except with His permission? He knows what is before them and what is behind them. They can not compass aught of His knowledge except as He wills. His Throne extends over the heavens and the earth, and He is never weary of preserving them for He is the Most High, the Great."

Light 24:35: *God is the Light of the heavens and the earth...*

See §7 below.

The universe is huge, seemingly infinite. Our sun is one among millions of stars in our galaxy and there are millions of similar galaxies that we can see with the available technology, so that our solar system is just a point inside another point at the universe scale.

On the other hand all these systems are subject to highly sophisticated laws and rules either at the large scale of the universe or at the infinitely small scale of matter elements, whose understanding is an ongoing and endless process:

The Forgiver 40:57
"Assuredly the creation of the heavens and the earth is a greater matter than the creation of men: Yet most people do not know."

The Cow 2:29
" It is He Who created for you all things that are on earth; Then turned He to the heaven, and perfected it as seven heavens. And He is Knower of all things."

Without going through any argumentations, when one is thinking about the Creation, it is natural to consider that this universe with its immensity and complexity needs someone, not only to have created it but to sustain it, 'concern' which also holds for our planet Earth whose exceptional conditions (temperature, oxygen, sun, vegetation, energy, ...) are all necessary for our life and existence :

The Creator 35:41
"It is God Who sustains the heavens and the earth, lest they cease (to function) ; and if they should fail, there is none to sustain them thereafter ; Verily He is Most Forbearing, Most Forgiving"

Cattle 6:99
" It is He Who sends down rain from the skies: with it We produce vegetation of all kinds ; from some We produce green crops, out of which We produce grain, heaped up (at harvest); out of the date-palm and its sheaths (or spathes) (come) clusters of dates hanging low and near ; and then there are gardens of grapes, and olives, and pomegranates, each similar in kind yet different in variety ; when they begin to bear fruit, feast your eyes

with the fruit and the ripeness thereof. Behold! in these things there are signs for people who believe."

The Prophets 21:30
"Do not those who deny the truth see that the heavens and the earth were one of piece, and We opened them out? And We made from water every living thing. Will they not believe?"

This need of a Sustainer is also that of a wise Master who is ruling the destiny of the world, of the creation, of everybody and everything in the universe. According to the Quran this is possible only if there is a unique God:

The Prophets 21:22
"If there were in them gods other than God, then they would have gone to ruin. So glory be to God, Lord of the Throne, He is high above their claims !"

Also and still according to the Quran, God should be extensively praised for His Creation, His wisdom, His grace and for being one and only one Lord and Sustainer of the world :

The Night Journey 17:111
"And say, 'Praise be to God, who begets no son, and has no partner in sovereignty, nor needs He any to protect Him from weakness, and magnify Him for His greatness and glory' "

In addition to the belief in God, Islam calls for the belief:
− in the Prophets as messengers of God; there are numerous Prophets mentioned in the Quran : Noah, Hud, Salih, Abraham, Loth, Ismael, Isaac, Jacob, Joseph, Chuaib, Moses, Jonas, Elisee, Jod, Jesus the Christ, the Apostles:
− in the Holy Books revealed: Quran and the books mentioned in it, the Torah, the Psalms, the Gospel. The Quran also indicates that these books have been subjected to some distortions.

— the existence of other creatures that human beings do not know in principle : angels and djins.
— the day of resurrection when human beings will rise from death and will be asked and rewarded for their actions and deeds.

The Quran points out that there is nothing strange that God had sent messengers in order to convey His message in various circumstances and by various means, such as providing a book of guidance that is revealed to a Prophet:

Jonah 10 10:2
"Is it a matter of wonderment to men that We have sent Our inspiration to a man from among themselves?- that he should warn mankind (of their danger), and give the good news to the Believers that they have before their Lord the lofty rank of truth. (But) say the Unbelievers: 'This is indeed an evident sorcerer!'"

4. Prayer (Salah) and remembrance of God

Prayer, considered as the most important duty for Muslims, formalizes the relationship between Man and his Creator and is cited in the beginning of the Quran:

The Cow 2:1-5
"A.L.M. This is the Book in which there is no doubt, a guidance for those who are mindful of God;
Who believe in the Unseen, are steadfast in prayer, and spend out of what We have provided for them ... and those are the successful."

And many other places, like:
The Wrapped One 73:20
"... and establish regular Prayer and give regular Charity."

4.1. General meaning

Literally, prayers mean solemn requests or expressions of worship to God. It is the possibility given to men:
- to ask God for help and guidance in different <u>aspects</u> of life: work, choices to be done, behaviour, etc.,
- to ask God forgiveness,
- to praise God and celebrate His glory.

4.2. Regular prayers in Islam: a duty in the best interest of Man

The daily prayers have to be accomplished five times a day: at dawn, noon, mid-afternoon, sunset and nightfall. The weekly prayer is accomplished on Friday at noon and contains a sermon which is devoted to remind or discuss moral values (such as the topics we discuss in this book) as well as various issues about life : family, social, religious, and other practical ones.

A prayer is composed of several units: two (dawn), three (sunset) or four (noon, mid-afternoon and nightfall). In each unit, the opening surah is recited first in addition to some other verses of the Quran. After this, expressions of praise and glory of God are said with some gestures (one genuflection and two prostrations) in recognition of the majesty and greatness of God as well as His grace; this symbolizes also humility and obedience of men to God. Personal prayers can also be formulated at this stage.

The first surah of the Quran, which is recited many times in regular prayers, illustrates this.The first part is concerned by the expression of praise and glory to God:

The Opening 1
"1 In the name of God, Most Gracious, Most Merciful.
2 Praise be to God, Lord of the worlds;

3 Most Gracious, Most Merciful;
4 Master of the Day of Judgment."

And the second part is devoted to asking for guidance :

5 You alone we worship; You alone we ask for help.
6 Show us the straight way,
7 The way of those on whom You Have bestowed Your Favours,
not those against whom there is anger, nor of those who go
astray."

The guidance is understood in a broad sense, regarding what we know, what we are concerned with and aware about, and also what we do not know and we are unaware about, having in mind that God is the All-knowing.

Prayer expresses also the wish to become closer to God, to show obedience. It shows humility of Man in the presence of God. Payer means also that men need constantly God for help and guidance. An opposite feeling would mean self-sufficiency, pride or arrogance, the true believer knows that he cannot claim, since he is aware of his weakness.

The surah 96 (The Clot) refers to this point. Man has been created in a very fragile and dependent state, as embryo and a baby, but when he acquires some power (which is provided by God in any case), he may be deceived by this (temporary) strength and is sometimes inclined to show some arrogance and self-sufficiency:

The Clot 96:1-8
"Read, in the name of your Lord, who created
He created man, out of a clot
Read! And your Lord is Most Generous
He Who taught by means of the pen,-
He Taught man what he never knew.
Nay, but man do transgress all bounds,

When he looks upon himself as self-sufficient.
Verily, to your Lord is the return (of all)."

The Romans 30:54
"*God is He Who created you weak, then after weakness gave you strength, then after strength gave you weakness and gray hair. He creates whatever He wills. He is the Omniscient, the Omnipotent.*"

Besides, prayer constitutes an opportunity for expressing praise and requests directly to God, the Master of human being destiny, without any intermediary.
Moreover, according to Quran, prayer enables humans to observe uprightness in behaviour, incites to virtue and good actions and restrains from immorality and evil:

The Spider 29:45
"*Recite what is revealed to you of the Book, and establish regular Prayer; for Prayer restrains from shameful and unjust deeds; and remembrance of God is the greatest (thing in life) without doubt. And God knows what you do.*"

Some rules of propriety are codified for prayers. In particular cleanliness is required and ablutions have to be done by washing hands, face and feet.

4.3. What to pray for ? The Quran teaches men some relevant prayers

Man is not always supposed to know what is worthwhile to ask, to pray or even to hope for. This requires a great deal of knowledge, experience and wisdom. It is remarkable that the Quran contains in some surah explicit examples of prayers which show what kind of request should matter for men. In in addition to the opening Surah, let us quote:

The Cow 2

"201- And there are some among them who say, 'Our Lord, give us goodness in this world, and goodness in the Hereafter, and guard us from the torment of the Fire.'"

"286- God does not burden any soul beyond its capacity. To its credit is what it earns, and against it is what it commits. 'Our Lord, do not condemn us if we forget or make a mistake. Our Lord, do not burden us as You have burdened those before us. Our Lord, do not burden us with more than we have strength to bear; and pardon us, and forgive us, and have mercy on us. You are our Lord and Master, so help us against the disbelieving people.'"

"286- On no soul does God Place a burden greater than it can bear. It gets every good that it earns, and it suffers every ill that it earns. (Pray:) 'Our Lord! Condemn us not if we forget or fall into error; our Lord! Lay not on us a burden Like that which You did lay on those before us; Our Lord! Lay not on us a burden greater than we have strength to bear. Blot out our sins, and grant us forgiveness. Have mercy on us. You are our Lord ; Help us against those who stand against faith.'"

The Family of Imran 2:8

Our Lord! Let not our hearts deviate now after You have guided us, but grant us mercy from Your Presence; for You are the Grantor of bounties without measure.

The Cave 18:10

Behold, the youths betook themselves to the Cave: they said, 'Our Lord! bestow on us Mercy from Yourself, and dispose of our affair for us in the right way!'

Some prayers of Prophets are mentioned for that purpose and also in order to illustrate the form as well as the content for requests in specific situations:

A Prayer of Abraham :
Abraham 14: 35-31

"*Remember Abraham said: 'O my Lord! make this city one of peace and security ; and preserve me and my sons from worshipping idols.'*"

"*O my Lord! they have indeed led astray many among mankind; He then who follows my (ways) is of me, and he that disobeys me,- but You are indeed Oft- forgiving, Most Merciful.*"

"*O our Lord! I have made some of my offspring to dwell in a valley without cultivation, by Your Sacred House; in order, O our Lord, that they may establish regular Prayer ; so fill the hearts of some among men with love towards them, and feed them with fruits ; so that they may be thankful.*"

"*O our Lord! truly You know what we conceal and what we reveal: for nothing whatever is hidden from God, whether on earth or in heaven.*"

"*Praise be to God, Who has granted unto me in old age Isma'il and Isaac ; for truly my Lord is He, the Hearer of Prayer!*"

"*O my Lord! make me one who establishes regular Prayer, and also (raise such) among my offspring O our Lord! and accept my Prayer.*"

"*O our Lord! cover (us) with Your Forgiveness - me, my parents, and (all) Believers, on the Day that the Reckoning will be established!*"

A prayer of Moses:
The Heights 7:155-156

"*And Moses chose seventy of his people for Our place of meeting ; when they were seized with violent quaking, he prayed:*

"O my Lord! if it had been Your will You could have destroyed, long before, both them and me: would You destroy us for the deeds of the foolish ones among us? this is no more than Your trial: by it You cause whom You will to stray, and You lead whom You will into the right path. You are our Protector: so forgive us and give us Your mercy; for You are the best forgiver."

"And ordain for us that which is good, in this life and in the Hereafter: for we have turned unto You."

A prayer of Job:
The Prophets 21:83-84
"And (remember) Job, when He cried to his Lord, 'Truly distress has seized me, but You are the Most Merciful of those that are merciful.'"
So We answered him: We removed the distress that was on him, and We restored his family to him, and doubled their number,- as a Grace from Ourselves, and a reminder for the worshipers.

A prayer of Jonah :
The Prophets 21:87-88
"And remember Jonah, when he departed in wrath: He imagined that We had no power over him! But he cried through the depths of darkness, 'There is no god but You: glory to You: I was indeed of the wrong doers !'
So We responded to him: and delivered him from distress: and thus do We deliver the faithful."

4.4. Prayer and invitation to careful reflection

According to Islam, God gives Man the possibility to pray, make requests about all issues, hopes, fears he may be concerned with (family, health, work, etc...).
It is important to note that Man is urged to make use of his intelligence in order to:
  – make precise the subjects of his prayers, his wishes, his

concerns ;
- think about the possible solutions, outcomes, etc. (if it is about some difficult problem for instance).

Afterwards he will be in better position to formulate relevant prayers / requests, asking God for help and guidance.
This is also related to the important concept of the trust in God and reliance on Him (Tawakkoul), that is; after having carefully thought about one's case, to rely on God, to have trust in Him, and to take the right steps forward:

The Family of Imran 3:159.
"Then, when you have taken a decision put your trust in God. For God loves the trusting."

This is an incitement to think carefully, identify the choices and take the right actions, which should be compatible with one's ethical values. Man is indeed urged to set up the principles that should guide his choices and actions. This is opposed to simply waiting for 'something from the sky', unless for situations where man has no power about the issue he is dealing with and is facing a situation beyond his capabilities: an example is the pray in a drought period.

4.5. In difficult times

Man may be facing difficult or very difficult situations and overwhelming events in his lifetime. When spiritual references are lacking, these situations lead to the well-known phenomena of anxiety, fear, and depression with sometimes suicidal tendencies. It is precisely at these moments that Man experiences his weaknesses and limits, whatever the strengths he had before (or he believed to have had). Man is therefore urged to remain aware of his weakness and that every strength he may have is provided by God, and that everything might be questioned the day after;

this is illustrated in several places in the Quran such as the story reported in the Cave 18:32-45:

The Cave 18:39
"Why did you not, as you went into your garden, say: 'God's will (be done)! There is no power but with God!"

In cases where the problems appear to be beyond Man's strength and capabilities, belief and prayer help him keep confident and consider that a problem, a crisis, however hard it may be for him, is easy for the Almighty God. The Quran gives guidance in these situations trough several verses, among them:

The Cow 2:153:
"O you who believe! seek help with patient perseverance and prayer; for God is with those who patiently persevere."

Divorce 65:2-3
"And for those who are mindful of God, He (ever) prepares a way out, And He provides for him from sources he never expected. And if any one puts his trust in God, He will suffice him. For God will surely accomplish his purpose: verily, for all things has God appointed a due proportion."

Solace 94:5-6:
"So, verily, with hardship, there is ease: Verily, with hardship there is ease."

Important is the prayer of Jonah cited above:
The Prophets 21:87-88 :
"There is no god but You: glory to You: I was indeed of the wrong doers !"
So We responded to him: and delivered him from distress: and thus do We deliver the faithful.

According to a saying of the Prophet, whenever a Man prays sincerely and humbly with this Jonah´s prayer, while being in very difficult situation, God will respond to his prayers and come to his rescue. The point is that the last sentence which mentions "*and thus do We deliver the faithful*", implies that this answer of God to Jonah who was in a desperate situation extends to those who truly believe in Him and express repentance. One can read this verse and many other verses without paying attention to this deduction; this is a simple example of the subtleties we could find in the reading of many parts of the Quran.

4.6. Asking forgiveness and its virtue

Asking God forgiveness for one's (and also others') sins and mistakes, some of which we are not aware of, is a part of the prescriptions about prayers in Islam.

The Quran emphasizes the highly beneficial effects of this prayer for forgiveness: first when correctly and sincerely performed it enables man to reform himself, to abandon sinful actions and behaviours and to improve his moral qualities. In addition to demanding to men to stand righteous, the Quran mentions in many places that by asking forgiveness and repentance, man would be provided help, favours and ways out in critical situations however complex they might be:

Noah 71: 10-12
"*And I said, 'Ask forgiveness from your Lord; for He is ever-Forgiving;*
He will send rain to you in abundance;
And Give you increase in wealth and sons; and bestow on you gardens and bestow on you rivers of flowing water."

Hud 11:3

"And seek the forgiveness of your Lord, and turn to Him in repentance; that He may grant you a good enjoyment, for a term appointed, and bestow His abounding grace on every bountiful one. But if you turn away, then I fear for you the retribution of an awful Day."

(See also the prayer of Jonah cited above.) It is reported that the Prophet said: "Glad tidings to those who find a lot of seeking forgiveness in the record of their deeds."

4.7. In situations of distress

The following verse talks about situations of distress when men need urgent support and tells us that God responds whenever He is prayed; we understand here a prayer with high sincerity, and belief with confidence that (only) God can provide a way out:

The Ant 27:62

"Or, Who answers to the distressed one when he calls on Him, and Who relieves his suffering, and makes you, mankind, inheritors of the earth? Can there be another god besides God? Little it is that you heed!"

After being rescued or relieved Man has to be sincere with God ; yet he is often inclined to forget and the following verses depict this:

Jonah 10:12

"When trouble touches a man, He implores Us in all postures- lying down on his side, or sitting, or standing. But when We have solved his trouble, he passes on his way as if he had never implored Us for a trouble that touched him! thus do the deeds of transgressors seem fair in their eyes!"

Jonah 10:22-23

"He it is Who enables you to traverse through land and sea; so that when you are on ships;- they sail with them with a favourable wind, and they rejoice thereat; then comes a stormy wind and the waves come to them from all sides, and they think they are being overwhelmed: they cry unto God, sincerely offering their duty unto Him saying, 'If You deliver us from this, we shall truly show our gratitude!'

But when He delivers them, behold! they transgress insolently through the earth in defiance of right! O mankind! your insolence is against your own souls,- an enjoyment of the life of the present ; and in the end, to Us is your return, and We shall show you the truth of all that you did."

While before being rescued, man was praying in desperate circumstances, he would, afterwards, explain the solution to his trouble in a factual way: the problem or the crisis was overcome because of this and that and the intervention of this or that side helped resolve the crisis.

Of course a solution would follow in general from objective causes and factors (as opposed to miracles) but the matter of fact is that when Man is in this situation of distress he has no power and no idea on the outcome or the way to overcome his problem; for the believer, it is precisely God who initiates the causes which were the origin of the happy outcome.

4.8. Remembrance of God and gratefulness

This means to glorify, praise, and express thanks to God, in particular during, but it is not limited to, prayer moments:

Iron 57:1

"Whatever is in the heavens and on earth celebrates the Praises and Glory of God; for He is the Exalted in Might, the Wise."

The Clans: 33:41-43
"O you who believe! Celebrate the praises of God, and do this often;
And glorify Him morning and evening.
He it is Who sends blessings on you, as do His angels, that He may bring you out from the depths of Darkness into Light ; and He is Full of Mercy to the Believers."

The Night Journey 17:44
"The seven heavens and the earth, and all beings therein, declare His glory: there is not a thing but celebrates His praise; And yet you do not understand their praises! Verily He is Forbearing, Most Forgiving!"

Man is also urged to express gratitude for all what is given to him and in general to Mankind:

The Night Journey 17:70
"We have honoured the sons of Adam; provided them with transport on land and sea; given them for sustenance things good and pure; and conferred on them special favours, above a great part of our creation."

How often are we thankful of being preferred to all the creatures on Earth? And of being created in the best conditions and with the best capabilities ?

The Fig 95:4
"We created man in the best design."

The Bees 16:78
"It is He Who brought you forth from the wombs of your mothers when you knew nothing; and He gave you hearing and sight and intelligence and affections ; that you may give thanks (to God)..."

Man has been placed on earth which has on one hand exceptional conditions insuring life and on the other hand it has a huge number of resources which were made available to Man : it suffices to think about the various sources of foods (vegetation, fish, …), of material goods : woods, raw materials (iron, silicon, …), sources of energy, or one may just look at the goods he has at home and recall that all these were built up from some material that has been made available for Man on Earth :

The Bees 16:13
"And the things on this earth which He has multiplied for you in varying colours (and qualities): verily in this is a sign for men who celebrate the praises of God (in gratitude)."

Signs Spelled out 41:10
"He set on the (earth), mountains standing firm, high above it, and bestowed blessings on the earth, and measure therein all things to give them nourishment in due proportion, in four Days, in accordance with (the needs of) those who seek (Sustenance)."

At a more personal level, one could (and should) realize that he is actually given many specific gifts and privileges, such as health, wealth, family, children, knowledge, position, etc., which are forgotten (often one becomes aware of such a privilege only when he loses it); man is incited to remember all these and to be thankful for that ; as an example the Quran cites a reminder of God to Jesus with this regard :

The Table 5:110
"110. When God will say, 'O Jesus son of Mary, recall My favour upon you and upon your mother, how I supported you with the Holy Spirit. You spoke to the people from the crib, as in maturity. How I taught you the Scripture and wisdom, and the Torah and the Gospel. And recall that you molded from clay the shape of a bird, by My leave, and then you breathed into it, and it became a

bird, by My leave. And you healed the blind and the leprous, by My leave; and you revived the dead, by My leave. And recall that I restrained the Children of Israel from you when you brought them the clear miracles. But those who disbelieved among them said, `This is nothing but obvious sorcery.'

Then will God say: "O Jesus the son of Mary! Recall My favour upon and upon your mother. Behold! I strengthened you with the holy spirit, so that you spoke to the people in childhood and in maturity. Behold! I taught you the Book and Wisdom, the Torah and the Gospel and behold! you made out of clay, as it were, the figure of a bird, by My leave, and you breathed into it and it became a bird by My leave, and you healed those born blind, and the lepers, by My leave. And behold ! you revived the dead by My leave. And behold! I did restrain the Children of Israel from violence to you when you showed them the clear Signs, and the unbelievers among them said: 'This is nothing but evident magic'"

Important : The Quran reminds the reader that God is the source of every gift, favour, including our children, work, wealth and even our daily occupations, etc., and that all these and other things that matter for everyone should not distract from His remembrance. He is the most worthy of that:

The Hypocrites 63:9
"O you who believe! Let not your riches or your children divert you from the remembrance of God. Whoever does that—these are the losers. "

Besides, we are also reminded that our possessions are in fact a trial for us :

Gathering 64:15 *"Your possessions and your children may be but a trial: but with God, is the highest reward"*

It is common to consider that this remembrance of God "open the eyes", enables one to stand lucid and that "by remembering God, He will remind you of what really matters to you".
Further verses pertaining to God's favours:

The Bees 16:18
"If you would count up the favours of God, never would you be able to number them: for God is Oft-Forgiving, Most Merciful."

The Bees 16:53
"And whatever blessings you have is from God."

5. Charity and spending for the needy: an instrument for human solidarity

Charity is the aim of giving money, food or other material goods, help, etc. to people in need. However, Islam and Quran give it a much wider meaning: helping the others, devoting one's time and energy, knowledge, giving advises and by extension all actions pertaining to the general interest, beginning with relatives and close neighbours, are considered as an integral part of the broad concept of spending for the needy (in the sequel we use the term 'spending' alone):

Iron 57:7
"Believe in God and His Messenger, and spend from what He has made you trustees heirs. For those of you who believe and spend will have a great reward."

The Cow 2:3
"This is the Book; in which there is no doubt, a guidance to those who are mindful of God ;
Who believe in the Unseen, are steadfast in prayer, and spend out of what We have provided for them;"

In fact, charity and spending can be classified in two types:
- The alms-giving (Zakat): which is a mandatory spending and its amount per year is 2.5% of one's asset (money in general) which has more than one year maturity. There are other rules for the calculation of the amounts. The 'Zakat' is to be given to the persons in need (with a priority to relatives, neighbours, orphans, and of course other priorities such as people with emergency needs for medical reasons, etc.).
- Voluntary spending : It is also an obligation even if it is qualified as voluntary ; the difference with the previous type is that there is no fixed amount for it, except the prescription to be balanced with this regard:

The Criterion 25:67
"Those who, when they spend, are not extravagant and not niggardly, but hold a just balance between those extremes."

Charity is a very important duty, which is repeatedly emphasized in the Quran, for instance:

The Cow 2:254
"O you who believe! Spend out of what We have provided for you, before the Day comes when no bargaining, nor friendship nor intercession. Those who deny are the wrong-doers."

In the last sentence, the reference "those who deny" seems to mean in this context "those who reject" the former·injunction about spending although it may be interpreted in a broad sense "Those who deny the truth". See also the verses 261 and sequel of the same Sura (The Cow).

The Story 28:77
"But ... do good to others as God has done good to you"

Charity is an expression of the love of neighbour and proscribes the temptation of selfishness which prevails quite often: it is not sufficient to say or consider that one loves his neighbour for the love of God, one has to be able to express this love in concrete situations, when the others are in need.

It represents an aspect of the faith: while the commercial acts consist of spending money for immediate material compensations (when one buys goods), charity consists of spending without an immediate compensation but in order to conform to a moral duty.

Nevertheless, the Quran highlights the huge compensations, rewards and blessings for those who generously accomplish this spending and charity:

Blessings in wealth:
The Cow 2:261
"The parable of those who spend their substance in the way of God is that of a grain of corn: it grows seven ears, and each ear Has a hundred grains. God gives manifold increase to whom He pleases. And God is All-Embracing, All-knowing."

Getting ease in one's issues and peace of mind:
The Night 92:5-7
"So he who gives in charity and fears God,
And in all sincerity testifies to the best,-
We will indeed smooth his way towards ease."

Most importantly is the reward that God will be well pleased with the believer as far as he is applying God's prescriptions.

Let us point out that some studies have actually shown that people who devote parts of their income, wealth, activity, time, etc. to helping people in need, do have higher satisfaction and delight levels in life and more motivations in their occupations (family, work, etc.).

6. Fasting (Sawm): a lever for moral improvement and righteousness

Fasting is the obligation of not eating or drinking during the days of Ramadan month from dawn to dusk. Fasting is prescribed for persons who are able to perform it. If it is not the case, for some reasons like old age, illness, or trip, then they are exempted from doing it.

The Cow 2:183
"O you who believe! Fasting is prescribed to you as it was prescribed to those before you, that you become righteous."

So the motivation mentioned in this verse refers to righteousness, which includes good deeds, morals and behaviours ; and one can understand that fasting is intended to help Man improve himself in this regard. Besides, fasting gives men:

- the opportunity to know and experience hunger and therefore the conditions poor people endure.
- each year the opportunity to spend a spiritual month (Ramadan is the month during which the Quran was revealed), breaking with the monotony of the daily life and material occupations which tend to shadow the spiritual side of Man.
- the possibility to comply even further with the prescriptions and values advocated and to enhance one's moral standards.

The highly beneficial effects of fasting on (physical and moral) health have been the subject of many studies. In particular, fasting gives the body a quite long period of rest which is very welcomed, as the excess in food is a serious issue and a source of many troubles and deceases. The following verse is very likely a reference to this aspect among others:

The Cow 2:184 :
" ... And it is better for you that you fast, if you only knew. "

7. The Pilgrimage (Hajj) to Mecca: a spiritual journey

It is a ritual required once in life time for those who can afford it. Mecca is considered by the Quran as « the mother city», and the Kaaba as the first place of worship made for men; according to the Quran it was initially built up by the Prophets Abraham and Ismael.

The Cow 196
"And complete the Hajj (Pilgrimage) and the Umra in the service of God."

The pilgrimage begins on the 8th of the last month of the lunar calendar (Dhou Al Hijja) and includes:
-   Going to the plain of Mina (near Mecca) and spending the night there ;
-   Spending the day, at least from noon to sunset in the plain of Arafat ;
-   Spending the night in the plain of Muzdalifa and returning to Mina where one has to stay 3 or 4 days during which a ritual in Jamarat consists of a symbolic stoning (of the devil, according to the common interpretation) ;
-   One has to go during these days or afterwards to the holy Mosque in Mecca and walking down seven times around the Kaaba and then walking seven times between the Safa and Marwa which were small mounts near the Kaaba.

In addition to being moments dedicated to worship and remembrance of God, this ritual is an expression of the attachment to the uniqueness (Tawhid) of God and loyalty to

Him, the only One worthy of worship, The Creator and Sovereign of the universe.

This loyalty is exemplified in the Quran by the Prophet Abraham whose faith and loyalty was demonstrated in extremely difficult circumstances; some of the ritual acts are symbolic of some episodes of Abraham's life.

The pilgrimage 22:26,

"*33-34 Behold! We gave the site, to Abraham, of the Sacred House, saying: Do not associate anything in worship with Me; and sanctify My House for those who compass it round, or stand up, or bow, or prostrate themselves.*

And proclaim the Pilgrimage among men: they will come to you on foot and on every kind of camel, lean on account of journeys through deep and distant mountain highways;

That they may witness the benefits provided for them, and celebrate the name of God, through the Days appointed, over the cattle which He has provided for them : then eat from it and feed the unfortunate poor.

Then let them complete the rites prescribed for them, perform their vows, and again circumbulate the Ancient House.

Such (is the Pilgrimage): whoever honours the sacred rites of God, for him it is good in the Sight of his Lord. Lawful to you for food in Pilgrimage are cattle, except those mentioned to you ; but shun the abomination of idols, and shun the word that is false

Being true in faith to God, and never assigning partners to Him ; if anyone assigns partners to God, is as if he had fallen from heaven and been snatched up by birds, or the wind had swooped (like a bird on its prey) and thrown him into a far- distant place."

The most important moment of the pilgrimage is the day spent in the Mount of Arafat; a long wait for millions of pilgrims wearing the same white habit which, according to some interpretations symbolizes the day of resurrection when all human beings will be gathered. This day is devoted to prayers, remembrance of God and asking forgiveness with of course reflection about man's destiny, past, present, future and hereafter.

There, the Prophet Mohammed gave his last sermon; here is some of his words:

"...O People! Just as you regard this month, this day, this city as sacred, so regard the life and property of everyone a sacred trust. Return the goods entrusted to you to their rightful owners. Hurt no one so that no one may hurt you. Remember that you will indeed meet your Lord, and that He will indeed reckon your deeds ... All mankind is from Adam and Eve, an Arab has no superiority over a non-Arab nor a non-Arab has any superiority over an Arab; also a White has no superiority over a Black nor does a Black has any superiority over a White except by righteousness [piety and good action]..."

The pilgrimage is a singular moment for detachment and reflection about one's destiny.

The Umra is another pilgrimage which can be done any time during the year and consists of going to the holy Mosque, walking down seven times around the Kaaba, praying and walking seven times between the Safa and Marwa.

2 Learning, Knowledge, Work and Good Deeds

1. The quest of knowledge and learning

Among the privileges and blessings granted to humankind, one should note the ability to think, learn, acquire knowledge, make reasoning and act, with highly evolved mind capacities which enables Man to treat very complex subjects in all domains.

The development of these abilities is itself dependent on the learning effort; and the first step to this end is to read, which means both to acquire the ability of reading (and writing) and regular reading (which implies learning) afterwards in order to get knowledge. It is remarkable that the very first revealed words of the Quran concerns this incitement to read:

The Clot / Read! 96:1-5
"Read, in the name of your Lord, who created
He created man, out of a clot
Read! And your Lord is Most Generous
He Who taught by means of the pen,-
He Taught man what he never knew."

After that we find in the Quran many exhortations to learn:

Taha 20:114
"... O my Lord! advance me in knowledge."

Along with many others which urge Man to use the reason and his reasoning capabilities:

The Family of Imran 3:190
"Behold! in the creation of the heavens and the earth, and the alternation of night and day,- there are indeed Signs for people of understanding."

The Romans 30:24
"And among His Signs, He shows you the lightning, by way both of fear and of hope, and He sends down rain from the sky and with it gives life to the earth after it is dead. Verily in that are Signs for those who make use of the reason."

Mind capabilities and learning have raised man to a position of responsibility on earth:
In the celebrate passage on the creation of Man, God gave Adam knowledge of the names which symbolise the definition of things and their classification (which is the first act in a scientific work) and has provided him with the senses and the above mentioned abilities. With these privileges, Man was given the responsibility on earth:

The Cow 2:30-33
"Behold, your Lord said to the angels: 'I will create a vicegerent on earth.' They said: 'Will You place therein one who will make mischief therein and shed blood?- while we do celebrate Your praises and glorify Your holy name?' He said: 'I know what you do not know.'

And He taught Adam the names of all things; then He placed them before the angels, and said: 'Tell me the names of these if you are right.'
They said: 'Glory to You, of knowledge We have none, save what You have taught us: In truth it is You Who are perfect in

knowledge and wisdom.'
He said: 'O Adam! Tell them their names.' When he had told
them, God said: 'Did I not tell you that I know the secrets of
heaven and earth, and I know what you reveal and what you
conceal?'"

Humans are ennobled and preferred to other creatures existing on
earth by their capabilities, among others, of learning and use of
reason:

The Night Journey 17:70
"We have honoured the sons of Adam, provided them with
transport on land and sea, given them for sustenance things good
and pure, and conferred on them special favours, above many of
those We created"

Reason and knowledge enable men to reinforce their spiritual
convictions:

The Angels 35:28
"Those truly fear God, among His Servants, who have
knowledge ; for God is Exalted in Might, Oft-Forgiving."

Also, reason and knowledge enable men:
  – to act and behave in a reasonable way according to the
    advocated values; observing these values and virtues is
    actually improved by the use of reason.
  – to develop their skills, to work better and make progress
    and achievements as much as possible in order to enhance
    their dignity.

The Quran has honoured knowledge, scientists and scholars; as
example, it is a pride for them that in the verse below, their
testimony value is placed just after that of God and Angels:

The Family of Imran 3:18
"There is no god but He: That is the witness of God, His angels, and those endowed with knowledge, standing firm on justice. There is no god but He, the Exalted in Power, the Wise."

These are some aspects highlighting the huge importance given by Islam and the Quran to the quest of knowledge, learning and reason, with their motivations and goals.

2. Work and deeds

These are understood as both the professional occupations and all other deeds, achievements that men can make according to their positions and possibilities.

Work and deeds: determinant of Man's standard and reward

The emphasis made by Islam and Quran is strong and even the reference to believers in the widely repeated sentence in the Quran "As for those who believe" is nearly always combined with the condition "and do righteous deeds", for instance:

The Cave 18:30
"As to those who believe and work righteousness, verily We shall not waste the reward of any who do good works."

This illustrates the concern that faith has (also) to be demonstrated through concrete actions whether it is about work, deeds, behaviours and morals.
According to the Quran, the assessment or judgement of every human will be done according to his works, deeds in this very wide sense:

The Earthquake 99:7-8:
Then shall anyone who has done an atom's weight of good, see it!
And anyone who has done an atom's weight of evil, shall see it.

Among the purpose of life: Who is the best in deed ?

And even the purpose of life itself is related to the fact that men are tried in their lifetime which of them is the best in deeds, conduct, etc.:

The Sovereignty 67:2:
"He Who created Death and Life, that He may try which of you is best in deed: and He is the Almighty, the Forgiving;"

This is of course according to what Man was given as conditions and possibilities:

Cattle 6:165
"It is He Who hath made you successors upon the earth: He has raised you in ranks, some above others: that He may try you in the gifts He has given you ; for thy Lord is quick in punishment, yet He is indeed Oft-forgiving, Most Merciful."

That is why Man is continuously urged in the Quran to work and make righteous deeds as much as he can according to his means and to make use of his intelligence to this end:

Repentance 9:105
"And say: 'Work : Soon will God observe your work, and His Messenger, and the Believers'"

The Family of Imran 3:30
"On the Day when every soul will find all the good it has done, and as for the evil it has done, it will wish they were far, far away

from them. And God is compassionate towards His servants."
The Bees 16:97
"Whoever works righteousness, man or woman, and has Faith, verily, We shall grant him a good life, and reward them according to the best of their actions."

Honesty in work

Islam advocates also sincerity and honesty at work and condemns all kinds of cheating and illicit gains; and everyone is urged to do what is required in work and meet his duties and responsibilities:

The Beneficient 55:9
"So establish weight with justice and fall not short in the balance."

Hud 11:85
"And O my people! give just measure and weight, nor withhold from the people the things that are their due commit not evil in the land with intent to do mischief."

Defrauding (The Cheats) 83:1-3
"Woe to those that deal in fraud,-
Those who, when they have to receive by measure from men, demand full measure,
But when they have to give by measure or weight to men, give less than due."

This command to be fair in every balance has a very wide sense, including all the transactions and relations in various domains: work be it professional or any other work, commercial and even in social relations: what you get or what you demand for yourself should be equivalent to counterpart you give according to what it is agreed; or in many situations, to give / receive in similar way if you are at the place of the other part. Let us quote this saying of

the Prophet:
"None of you [truly] believes until he loves for his brother that which he loves for himself."

This principle is common in the other religions and believes; if it is properly understood and applied by people, human relations and condition will be considerably improved.

3. Work of reflection and use of reason

This is a line of conduct advocated throughout the Quran in various situations: before acting, or believing something, to think carefully; sometimes this requires significant effort of reflection and this is crucial in many situations: it is known that even in learning processes, this work of reflection makes a great difference between people. This is opposed to the quick acceptance of ideas and facts that are either not true or not fully understood (naïve behaviour). We see in the Quran expressions like:

The Cow 2:111
"... *Produce your proof if you are truthful."*

As an example, the story of Moses talks about the quick acceptance by the people of Egypt's Pharaoh of the arguments (or non-arguments) of the later, and their obedience to him while he was wrong:

The Ornaments of Gold 43:51-54
"*And Pharaoh proclaimed among his people, saying: 'O my people! Does not the dominion of Egypt belong to me, (witness) these streams flowing underneath my (palace)? What! see ye not then?*
Am I not better than this (Moses), who is a contemptible wretch

and can scarcely express himself clearly?
Then why are not gold bracelets bestowed on him, or (why) come
(not) with him angels accompanying him in procession?'
Thus did he make fools of his people, and they obeyed him: truly
were they a people rebellious (against God)."

In that sense, Man is urged to make the biggest use of reason and
critical reflection (see also the argumentations of Abraham in :
Cattle 6:74-83 and The Prophets 21:51-71, The Poets 26:69-89).

Besides, this incitement to reflection, is repeatedly emphasized in
many situations like :

The Family of Imran 3:190
Behold! in the creation of the heavens and the earth, and the
alternation of night and day,- there are indeed Signs **for men of**
understanding,-
Romans *30:21*
And among His Signs is this, that He created for you mates from
among yourselves, that you may dwell in tranquillity with them,
and He has put love and mercy between your : verily in that are
Signs **for people who reflect.**

This work of reflection remains indeed one of the most powerful
means to the success in every field of life.

3 Moral values in the Quran

*"God commands justice, doing good, and generosity towards
relatives, and He forbids immorality, and abomination and
transgression. He advises you, so that you may take heed."*
The Bee 16:90

Islam and Quran advocate a set of moral values regarding human
behaviour and relationship at individual and collective levels;
these morals are announced throughout the Text either as basic
principles or as rules deduced from narrative cases. Among them:

Uprightness

The Dunes 46:13
*"Those who say,'Our Lord is God,' then lead a righteous life—
they have nothing to fear, nor shall they grieve."*

Hud 11:112
*"Therefore stand firm in the straight Path as you have been
commanded."*

One wonders what does this concept of righteousness mean in
practice. This is a good point of reflection for everyone when
thinking about the standards one should meet. In fact this concept
includes the following qualities and values:

Kindness with and honouring Parents

The Night Journey 17:23
"Your Lord has decreed that you worship none but Him, and that you be kind to parents. Whether one or both of them attain old age in your life, say not to them a word of contempt, nor repel them, but address them in terms of honour."

Equity and justice: "... Be just, that is next to piety"

Cattle 6:153
"whenever you speak, speak justly, even if a near relative is concerned"

The Table 5:8
"O you who believe! stand out firmly for God, as witnesses to fair dealing, and let not the hatred of others to you make you swerve to wrong and depart from justice. Be just; that is next to piety: and fear God. For God is well-acquainted with all that you do."

Women 4:58
"God commands you to render back the trusts to those to whom they are due; And when you judge between people, that you judge with justice: Verily how excellent is the teaching which He gives you! For God is all-Hearing, all-Seeing."

Good words (in communications): "A goodly word like a goodly tree"

Abraham 14:24-27
"Do you not see how God sets forth a parable? - A goodly word like a goodly tree, whose root is firmly fixed, and its branches are high in the sky.
It brings forth its fruit at all times, by the leave of its Lord. So God sets forth parables for men, in order that they may receive admonition.
And the parable of an evil Word is that of an evil tree: It is torn up by the root from the surface of the earth: it has no stability.

God will establish in strength those who believe, with the word that stands firm, in this world and in the Hereafter; but God will leave, to stray, those who do wrong and God does what He wills."

The Cow 2:83

"... and speak kindly to (all) the people."

Women 4:148

"God does not like bad words to be made in public, except when one is treated with injustice; For God is all-Hearing, all-Seeing"

Women 4:86

"When a (courteous) greeting is offered you, meet it with a greeting still more courteous, or (at least) of equal courtesy. God takes careful account of all things."

When Moses was sent to Pharaoh, he was told (by God) to speak gently to him (despite the mischief of Pharaoh)

Taha 20:44

"But speak gently to him, perchance he may take warning or fear (God)."

So if one is told to speak mildly even to a person like Pharaoh (at least in the beginning), one should obviously be courteous and kind in his communication with people in general.

Good deeds : " ... and do good deeds so that you may succeed"

The pilgrimage 22:77

" ... and do good deeds so that you may succeed"

The Family of Imran 3:30

"On the Day when every soul will find all the good it has done ..."

The Prophets 21:73

"And We made them leaders, guiding people by Our Command, and We sent them inspiration to do good deeds, to establish regular prayers, and to practise regular charity; and they

constantly served Us."
The Prophets *21:90*
"... they [Zakaria, his wife and John] used to vie one with the other in good deeds and to call upon Us hoping and fearing and humble themselves before Us."

Honouring one's commitments and honesty : *"O you who believe! fulfil your obligations"*

The Table 5:1
"O you who believe! fulfil your obligations"

In this verse the term "obligations" translates the term "Okoud" plural of "Akd" which is also the Arabic term of 'Contract'.

The Night Journey 17:34
"... and fulfil your engagement, for every engagement shall be questioned about"
The Believers 23:1-8
"Successful are the believers ... Those who faithfully observe their trusts and engagements."

The previous verses talk specifically about fulfilment of Man's engagements and duties in general as well as this quality of honesty, see also Women 4:58 quoted above.

Modesty : *"... Nor walk on the earth with insolence"*

The Criterion 25:63
"And the servants of (God) Most Gracious are those who walk on the earth in humility, and when the ignorant address them, they say, 'Peace!'";
The Night Journey 17:37
"Nor walk on the earth with insolence, for you cannot rend the earth asunder, nor reach the mountains in height."

We all know the temptations of pride and arrogance; these verses remind man to be aware of his limitations despite the feeling of self-sufficiency, which cannot be sustainable; this incitement to modesty is valid for both man's relationships to others and man's internal feelings toward himself and his existence:

The Romans 30:9
"Do they not travel through the earth, and see what was the end of those before them? They were superior to them in strength ; they tilled the soil and populated it in greater numbers than these have done ; there came to them their Messengers with Clear Signs - Which they rejected, to their own destruction. It was not God Who wronged them, but they wronged their own souls"

Gratitude : "... *Be thankful to Me"*

The Cow 2:152
"Then remember Me, I will remember you. Be thankful to Me, and do not be ungrateful to Me."

Mercy and compassion : "... *and enjoin one another deeds of kindness and compassion"*

The reward one can expect is of the same nature as one's deed : a person who helps another in his illness or saves a life from death, or who generally is kind to people, animals etc., is of course likely to expect mercy from God when he is in need. On the opposite side, consider another person who could do good or help people in need but does not care about, and have no concern about the others; does he deserve kindness and mercy like the former one ? This law is expressed in verses like:

The City 90:17-18
"...Then will he be of those who believe, and enjoin one another patience, (constancy, and self-restraint), ***and enjoin one another***

deeds of kindness and compassion.
Such are the Companions of the Right Hand."

The Heights 7:55-56
"Call on your Lord with humility and in private. for God does not like the transgressors.
Do no mischief on the earth, after it has been set in order, but call on Him with fear and longing (in your hearts),
*for the **Mercy of God is (always) near to those who do good.***"

Moderation : " ... *And do not commit excess"*

The Cow 2:143
"Thus, have We made of you a moderate community justly balanced"
The Quran urges people to stand moderate and avoid excesses in everything ; this includes all human behaviours, concerning consumption, relationship to the others, etc., and is exemplified in verses like the following :

Cattle 6:141
*"It is He Who produces gardens, with trellises and without, and dates, and tilth with produce of all kinds, and olives and pomegranates, similar (in kind) and different (in variety): eat of their fruit in their season, but render the dues that are proper on the day that the harvest is gathered. **And do not commit excess: for God does not like those who commit excess.***"

Tolerance between men and communities, Equality between men, Open-mindedness

The Apartments 49:13
*"O mankind! We created you from a male and a female, and made you into nations and tribes, that you may know each other. Verily the most honoured of you in the sight of God is **the most***

righteous of you. And God is All-Knowing, All-Aware."

Prescription of good and prohibition of the reprimanded actions

The Family of Imran 3:104
"Let there arise out of you a community inviting to all that is good, enjoining what is right, and forbidding the evil. These are the successful."

Patience: " *for God is with those who patiently persevere"*

The Cow 2:153
"O you who believe! seek help with patient perseverance and prayer; for God is with those who patiently persevere."
The Cow 2:177
"... and to be firm and patient, in pain and adversity, and in times of danger. Such are the people of truth, the God-fearing."

Quest of reconciliation in case of conflicts

The Apartments 49:9
"If two parties among the Believers fall into a quarrel, make peace between them."

Prohibition of mockery, of consultations and gossips which harm other people

The Apartments 49:11
"O you who believe! Let not some men among you laugh at others: It may be that the latter are better than the former ; Nor let some women laugh at others: It may be that the latter are better than the former ; Nor defame nor be sarcastic to each other, nor call each other by offensive nicknames ; Ill-seeming is a name connoting wickedness, to be used of one after he has

believed: And those who do not desist are indeed doing wrong."
The Apartments 49:12

"... O you who believe! Avoid suspicion as much as possible ; for suspicion in some cases is a sin. And do not spy on each other behind their backs nor shall you backbite one another."
Women 4:114

"There is no good, in most of their secret talks, except if one exhorts to a deed of charity or justice or conciliation between men. To anyone who does this, seeking the good pleasure of God, We shall soon give a reward of the highest value."

Forgiveness: "... let them forgive and overlook, do you not wish that God should forgive you?"

Light 24:22
"... let them forgive and overlook, do you not wish that God should forgive you? For God is Most Forgiving, Most Merciful."

Restraint and Retention of resentment : "Those ... who restrain anger, and pardon people ; for God loves the doers of good"

The Family of Imran 133-134
"Be quick in the race for forgiveness from your Lord, and for a Garden whose width is that of the whole of the heavens and of the earth, prepared for the righteous,
Those who spend freely, whether in prosperity, or in adversity; who restrain anger, and pardon people ; for God loves the doers of good;"

Proscription of prejudice

The Apartments 49:6
"O you who believe! If a wicked person comes to you with any news, you shall first investigate, lest you harm people unwittingly, and afterwards become regretful for what you have done.

The private Apartments 49:12 *op. cit.*"
Respect of human life and its sacredness

The Table 5:32
"... *On that account: We ordained for the Children of Israel that if any one killed a person - unless it be for murder or for spreading mischief in the land - it would be as if he had killed the whole of mankind: and if any one saved a life, it would be as if he saved the life of the whole of mankind"*

Liberty and Freedom

The above mentioned incitement of the Quran to use reason, to think, work etc. implies the human freedom and men's responsibilities regarding their actions:

Repentance 9:105
"*And say: "Work righteousness"*

No restriction has been imposed on freedom except that of not harming the others or undermining their rights (for instance in family or social affairs):

The Cow 2:275
"... *but God has permitted trade and forbidden usury...*"
The Congregation 62:10
"*And when the Prayer is finished, then you may disperse through the land, and seek of the Bounty of God: and celebrate the Praises of God often: that you may be successful."*

In the last verse "Seek the Bounty of God" is interpreted as an incitement to undertake all actions to earn one's living: work, trade, entrepreneurship, etc.

Prohibition of adultery

The Night Journey 17:32
"And do not come near unto adultery: for it is an abomination and an evil way."

Solidarity

Repentance 9:60
"Alms are for the poor and the needy, and those employed to administer the funds; for those whose hearts have been reconciled to Truth; for those in bondage and in debt; in the cause of God; and for the wayfarer: this is an ordinance from God, and God is full of knowledge and wisdom."

Mutual advice

Time 103:1-3
"By the declining day, Verily Man is in loss,
Except such those who have Faith, and do righteous deeds, and join together in the mutual advice of Truth, and of Patience and Constancy."

Reformation : *"God does not change men's condition unless they change their inner selves"*

The Sun 91:9
"… the one who purifies and reform his soul succeeds"

This verse concerns the reformation effort that one should make for himself: assessment, recognition of one's mistakes and shortcomings, self-criticism and working on correcting one's thoughts, attitudes, etc.

The following verse concerns the reformation effort that ought to be continuously undertaken, and the verse can be read in two directions: If people are facing some serious issues, they have first to work and take the right steps to change their inner conditions and the factors that are at the origin of their troubles; this work has to be done with the necessary honesty, rigour and good will ; and by doing so they will have the support of God. This verse points out that people can not merely ask God for improving their conditions while they fail to perform the reformation work and to take actions which are within their area of responsibility.

In the other direction, blessings bestowed on people are maintained as long as they stand righteous and are worthy of these favours, which is valid at individual and collective levels:

The Thunder 13:11
"Verily, God does not change men's condition unless they change their inner selves"

Let us quote here Muhammad Asad's Translation comment on this verse: "This statement has both a positive and a negative connotation: i.e., God does not withdraw His blessings from men unless their inner selves become depraved (cf. 8:53), just as He does not bestow His blessings upon wilful sinners until they change their inner disposition and become worthy of His grace. In its wider sense, this is an illustration of the divine law of cause and effect (sunnat Allah) which dominates the lives of both individuals and communities, and makes the rise and fall of civilizations dependent on people's moral qualities and the changes in "their inner selves"."

In public affairs, Islam advocates the principle of dialogue and consultation.

Consultation 42:38
"Those ... who conduct their affairs by mutual Consultation ..."

The Family of Imran 3:159
"... and consult them in affairs. Then when you have taken a decision put your trust in God. For God loves the trusting."

From this incitement, made in this case to the Prophet, we can draw a general principle. It calls to take into account the views of everyone, and study carefully the case we are concerned with, which would clarify it and make easy the decisions to be considered : the expression « if you have taken a decision » may be read « when you are convinced about some choice » : the decision is likely to be well-founded and the conviction is reinforced as much as the consensus reached about the subject is wide. A problem may be a complex one and has many sides that may not be considered by a person alone, who will necessarily view the issue from his own angle, according to his own background; and therefore taking into account the views of the others, who may be experts of the subject dealt with or representative of the collective views is likely to insure the reach of the appropriate decisions and the best results.

This joins the concepts of pluralism and democratic societies, to mention the terms used in the present time. The organization and implementation details (legislative and executive bodies, regional and local affairs, etc.) are left to Man and are subject to texts like constitutions, fundamental laws, laws, etc. They are supposed to evolve over time and are dependent on nations and cultures.

These ethic principles are nowadays commonly admitted and may be considered as universal; their aim is to insure peaceful life and coexistence among people in all situations, despite their differences at all levels, beginning from family life, to relations at collective or international levels. The difficulty lies of course in their application in all situations; one can often be convinced of some rules of conduct but does not succeed to comply with them. The demand is precisely to do the best in order to conform to these high standards ; this requires education, internal conviction, self-assessment regarding these rules and learning from one's own and others' experiences and ... struggle against pride.

Indeed, one has to show modesty and not consider oneself above errors and shortcomings; this last condition seems to be difficult, and requires sometimes a deep internal work to overcome what could be considered as a common psychological obstacle : to be able to admit that we are wrong and to say it ; this way is, in turn, a very simple way to resolve many conflicts and crises; but pride is usually a big problem and prevents one from acknowledging his mistakes and from engaging a self-criticism.

In this endeavour, to improve our behaviour and standard, one has to be aware of this requirement of a continuous perfection work; some scholars (like Al Ghazali in his Revival of Religious Sciences) had also talked long time ago about acquiring some qualities by 'exercises' : for instance those related to behaviour: how to show restraint, to contain anger; how to show forbearance, forgiveness, etc.

Let us end this chapter with this verse which summarizes a big part of the Islamic moral values to the extent that the Caliph Umar Ibn Abd al-Aziz (681-720) advocated to mention it at the end of the sermon of each Friday prayer:

The Bee 16:90
"God commands justice, doing good, and generosity towards relatives, and He forbids immorality, and abomination and transgression. He advises you, so that you may take heed."

4 Conception of the World

The Quran provides men some basic information and ideas to help them in their reflection about existence, creation, the Creator, man's destiny, the role of human beings, and the purpose of life.

1. The Creator, Almighty God

The belief in one God was discussed previously and Islamic basic principle is a rigorous monotheism: God is one and unique. All kinds of 'association' of another divinity are strongly rejected.

Although the Quran indicates that God has no resemblance with what men could imagine, it provides some indications on the attributes of God : the Quran quotes some of them: the Creator, the Omnipresent, the Almighty, the Wise, the Lenient (Indulgent), the Most Merciful, the Most Gracious, the Sovereign. He is the Sustainer of the universe and all the creatures.

Exile 59:22-24
"He is God, than Whom there is no other god; -Who knows all things both secret and open; He, Most Gracious, Most Merciful.

He is God, than Whom there is no other god;- the Sovereign, the Holy One, the Source of Peace, the Granter of security, the Supreme, the Almighty, the Most Powerful, the Most Dignified. Glory to God! (High is He) above the partners they attribute to Him.

He is God, the Creator, the Initiator, the Designer. To Him belong the Most Beautiful Names: whatever is in the heavens and on earth, do declare His Praises and Glory: and He is the Exalted in Might, the Wise"

Iron 57:1-6
"Whatever is in the heavens and on earth,- let it declare the Praises and Glory of God: for He is the Exalted in Might, the Wise.

To Him belongs the dominion of the heavens and the earth: It is He Who gives Life and Death; and He has Power over all things.

He is the First and the Last, the Evident and the Immanent: and He has full knowledge of all things.

He is Who created the heavens and the earth in Six Days, and is moreover firmly established on the Throne of Authority. He knows what enters within the earth and what comes forth out of it, what comes down from heaven and what mounts up to it.

And He is with you wheresoever you may be. And God sees well all that you do.

To Him belongs the dominion of the heavens and the earth: and all affairs are referred back to God.
He merges Night into Day, and He merges Day into Night; and He has full knowledge of the secrets of all hearts."

Quran gives also an idea about the reality of God, in the famous verse:

Light 24:35 :
"God is the Light of the heavens and the earth. The Parable of His Light is as if there were a Niche and within it a Lamp: the Lamp enclosed in Glass: the glass is like a brilliant star: Lit from

a blessed Tree, an Olive, neither of the east nor of the west,
whose oil would almost illuminate, though fire has not touched it:
Light upon Light! God guides whom He wills to His Light: God
sets forth Parables for men: and God is Knower of all things."

There are many other verses about the majesty of God and His
universal presence be it explicit or implicit, with relation to all
what regards the world and who or what is therein, for instance:

Hud 11:123
"To God do belong the unseen (secrets) of the heavens and the
earth, and to Him goes back every affair ; then worship Him, and
put your trust in Him: and your Lord is not unmindful of aught
that you do."

Cattle 6:59
"With Him are the keys of the unseen, the treasures that none
knows but He. He knows whatever there is on the earth and in the
sea. Not a leaf doth fall but with His knowledge ; there is not a
grain in the darkness (or depths) of the earth, n or anything fresh
or dry (green or withered), but is (inscribed) in a record clear (to
those who can read)."

Cattle 6:95-99
"6:95 It is God Who causes the seed-grain and the date-stone to
split and sprout. He causes the living to issue from the dead, and
He is the one to cause the dead to issue from the living. That is
God, then how are you deluded away from the truth?"

"6:96 He it is that cleave the day-break (from the dark) ; He
makes the night for rest and tranquillity, and the sun and moon
for the reckoning (of time). Such is the judgement and ordering of
the Exalted in Power, the Omniscient."

"6:97 It is He Who makes the stars (as beacons) for you, that you

may guide yourselves, with their help, through the dark spaces of land and sea ; We detail Our signs for people who know. "

"6:98 It is He Who has produced you from a single person ; here is a place of sojourn and a place of departure. We detail Our signs for people who understand. "

"6:99 It is He Who sends down rain from the skies, with it We produce vegetation of all kinds, from some We produce green (crops), out of which We produce grain, heaped up (at harvest); out of the date-palm and its sheaths (or spathes) come clusters of dates hanging low and near ; and then there are gardens of grapes, and olives, and pomegranates, each similar in kind yet different in variety ; when they begin to bear fruit, feast your eyes with the fruit and the ripeness thereof. Behold! in these things there are signs for people who believe. "

2. Creation and Genesis of the world

The Quran mentions the creation of the earth and the heavens in six days (to be understood as six periods), which joins the indications of the Old Testament, but there are some differences and further information cited at several places of the Text :

Qaf 50:38
"We created the heavens and the earth and all that is between them in Six Days, and no weariness touched Us. "

The creation of Man with Adam and then Eve, and the designation of him as vicegerent in the earth, assigning to him a huge responsibility, with reference to the abilities he was granted and the preference he is given among many other creatures:

69

The Cow 2:30-38
"Behold, your Lord said to the angels: "I will create a vicegerent on earth ...
...And He taught Adam the names of all things ..."

3. The Quran: A spiritual book providing senses to life and existence

Answers and other elements are given about these deep questions as in the following verses:

The Windowing winds 51:56
"I created the jinn and humankind only that they might worship Me."

The Sovereignty 67:1-2
"Exalted is He in Whose hands is the sovereignty ; and He has power over all things ;
Who has created Death and Life, that He may try which of you is best in deed: and He is the Almighty, the Forgiving;"

In the first verse the term worship is to be understood in a wider sense : obedience that includes various prescriptions : work, performing good deeds (spending, etc.), moral rules (righteousness, justice, humility, patience, tolerance, etc.) as well as acts of prayers, remembrance of God, etc.

The Quran is both a spiritual and practical book. As a spiritual book it aims to provide information giving sense to life, to existence, to Man's actions. Without such a reference, and this quest for the sense to existence, one would feel that life is vain and purposeless; a common feeling when one witnesses situations of pain, sorrow, death or mourning.

Some people may show a sort of self-sufficiency, or strength in such circumstances, and would think that they are in no need of a spiritual side to lead their lives; but this is a pride that no one is in position to hold. As soon as the same person would face a desperate situation undermining his life, he may change his views and discover the truth of his (past) strength.

The Quran contains continuous reminders and warnings about these facts. We are always reminded to be cautious and not be deceived by our current state of apparent strength, nor by life in general; there will be an end to everything :

The Creator 35:5

"O men! Certainly the promise of God is true. Let not then this present life deceive you, nor let the Chief Deceiver deceive you about God."

And that the hereafter should matter for Man, while pointing out that this is not incompatible with the work and strive in the present life. On the contrary, Man is urged to work as much as he can, to make the best achievements he could in this life in order to get the best reward therein and in the hereafter.

The Story 28: 77

"But seek, with the (wealth) which God has bestowed on thee, the Home of the Hereafter, nor forget your portion in this world and do good to others, as God has been good to you."

According to this, the Quran is, as it mentions, an enlightenment of the life of people, in providing them lasting motivations for acting and working righteousness, and showing them what is right and what is wrong, whence the other name of this sacred book : Al Furqan, that is the Criterion (of distinguishing between right and wrong, etc.) :

The Table 5:15-16

"... *There has come to you from God a (new) light and a perspicuous Book,-*

Wherewith God guides all who seek His good pleasure to ways of peace and safety, and leads them out of darkness, by His will, unto the light,- guides them to a path that is straight."

Women 4:174

"*O mankind! verily there has come to you a convincing proof from your Lord. For We have sent unto you a light (that is) manifest."*

Iron : 57:28

"*O you that believe! Be God-mindful , and believe in His Messenger, and He will bestow on you a double portion of His Mercy: He will provide for you a Light by which you shall walk (straight in your path), and He will forgive you (your past): for God is Oft- Forgiving, Most Merciful."*

The Criterion 25:1

"*Blessed is He who sent down the criterion (Al-Furqan) to His servant, that it may be an admonition to all creatures."*

4.Glad tiding for the righteous and warning for the evil-doers

The rules announced to students in a class contain motivations, encouragements, rewarding those who are engaged in work and as for those who show no care for their duties, the result would be undoubtedly a failure in the exams. In our societies there are also systems of reward for those who work hard, and are devoted in their jobs (in enterprises, institutions etc.) and also a system of retributions for the evil-doers (penal, civil code, etc.).

In the case of the Quran, it is about the assessment of a Man for all his deeds, behaviours, sayings, etc. The message is that of hope, good news, tremendously good news for the righteous according to their deeds.

Obviously, the message cannot be limited to that : in the human society, unfortunately not all people are righteous. There are also corrupted people, thieves, criminals, murderers, etc. What would be the message toward these people? The Quran contains warnings, severe warnings of punishments to the evil-doers, especially those who do not repent and persist in their misbehaviour but also an incitement to repentance and signs of hope for God's forgiveness under conditions.

The careful reader of the Quran will note a remarkable balance between the insisting messages of hope of forgiveness and urge to repentance for the sinners on one hand and the repeating messages of severe warning to them on the other hand.

5. Responsibility of Man on Earth

There are many parts of the Quran which remind Man about his responsibilities on earth, in particular that of insuring the good living environment for him and other creatures:

The Heights 7:56:
"Do no mischief on the earth, after it has been set in order"

Many of the environmental issues are originated in the excesses committed towards nature, regarding the consumption while a significant part of the production is wasted, etc.

Cattle 6:141
"... And do not commit excess: for God does not like those who commit excess."

The verses about the creation of Man as a vicegerent on earth imply obviously his global responsibility:

The Cow 2:30-38
" *Behold, your Lord said to the angels: "I will create a vicegerent on earth ...*
...And He taught Adam the names of all things..."

All these are invitations to think about central existential questions ; this reflection should allow to provide a sense to life for everyone, that goes beyond the material aspects and current affairs of life ; these pure material sides lose their purpose, in the absence of a spiritual reference for man, whenever the reality of death is taken into account.

Reading the Quran provides an insight on these subjects which are either addressed directly or stand in the background of the whole Text. Discussions and reflections about these issues are free and the use of reason and all human intelligence are recommended for that purpose. This has given rise to fruitful and prolific works about philosophy, logic, science, since the dawn of Islam, with several schools of thoughts. Yet these philosophical studies have to be revisited from a modern perspective, and there are valuable works in this regard, some of which are specifically concerned with scientific facts mentioned in the Quran.

5 Tolerance in Islam

Tolerance is one of the fundamental values of Islam, at individual, collective and religious levels. Several aspects have to be emphasized in this respect:

Diversity in the world reflects a God's will

According to Islam, the diversity of human beings, at ethnic, linguistic, cultural level, is among the signs of God and reflects His will:

The Romans 30:22
"And among His Signs is the creation of the heavens and the earth, and the variations in your languages and your colours."

Life in this environment of diversity should therefore go through mutual aid and mutual knowledge as well as open-mindedness:

The Apartments 49:13
"O mankind! We created you from a male and a female, and made you into nations and tribes, that you may know each other. Verily the most honoured of you in the sight of God is the most righteous of you. And God is All-Knowing, All-Aware."

Recognition by Islam of the monotheist religions, Judaism and Christianity

The differences in monotheist beliefs establish the will of the

Creator and if He had so wished, He would have made only one community from the beginning. This idea is mentioned many times in the Quran:

The Table 5:48
"And *We sent to you the Scripture in truth, confirming the scripture that came before it, and superseding it : so judge between them by what God has revealed, and do not follow their vain desires, diverging from the Truth that has come to you. To each among you have we prescribed a law and an open way. If God had so willed, He would have made you a single community, but He wishes to test you in what He has given you: so compete in virtuous deeds. The goal of you all is to God; it is He that will show you the truth of the matters in which you dispute;"*

The Cow 2:62
"Those who believe in the Quran, those who follow the Jewish scriptures, and the the Christians, and the Sabians - any who believe in God and the Last Day, and work righteousness,- on them shall be no fear, nor shall they grieve."

The Pilgrimage 22:17
"Those who believe in the Quran, those who follow the Jewish scriptures, and the Sabians, Christians, Magians, and Polytheists,- God will judge between them on the Day of Judgment: for God is witness of all things"

In the verse 5:48 and others e.g. 22:17, it is stated that God is the Only Judge between people in faith matters, as everyone considers that his faith or belief or unbelief is the truth.

No Compulsion in religion

The adoption by Islam of the principle: *"Let there be no compulsion in religion" (The Cow 2:256)* is fundamental. It means that one must not require people to embrace a given religion, and that any belief in a religion is a valid one only if it follows from a personal will and conviction without being under constraint.

The following verse reinforce this principle of freedom in faith and beliefs:

The Cave 18:29
"Say, 'The truth is from your Lord': Then whoever wills, let him believe, and whoever wills let him reject it."

The previous principles show that, fourteen centuries ago, Islam has called for the highest values of tolerance, mutual understanding and open-mindedness. In fact the reality of Islam has no link with the image often conveyed about this religion in some circumstances where violence acts are mixed with religious considerations.

Moderation

Islam is also a religion of moderation in every respect: thought, relationships, behaviours, attitudes, not forgetting worship, which is summarized in this verse:

The Cow 2:143
"Thus, have We made of you a moderate community justly balanced".

In the Arabic Text, the Quran uses the term "wassat", rather close to "middle" than the term moderate used previously, but it includes also this notion of moderation. Let us mention this symbolic fact, that this verse no:143 is ranked precisely at the medium of the surah 2 (The Cow) which contains 286 verses.

Islam has no link with the violence phenomena associated with its name

There are actually verses and parts of the Quran dealing with situations of conflict, which when read or presented out of their historical context might lead to false deductions, mixing Islam and Quran with some violence injunctions; this misinterpretation is sometimes used, knowingly or by ignorance by various sides either to serve specific goals and agenda or to convey a negative image of this religion.

In these circumstances, confusions and prejudices prevail and Islam becomes also a victim of the passions, madness of some people.

In order to have the right view on this, a brief historical overview is in order. Islamic Preach had begun in 610 CE by the Prophet Muhammed in Mecca ; he soon had to face, with his first followers, hostility and persecutions.

Early Muslims had stood with peaceful attitude towards their tribe in this turmoil for a period of 13 years. This situation of weakness culminated with their emigration to the city of Yathrib (Madinah) and also with the attempt to kill the Prophet, which is reported in the Quran:

Spoils of wars 8:30
"Remember how those who bent in denying the Truth plotted against you, to keep you in bonds, or slay you, or expel you. They plot and plan, and God too plans; but the best of planners is God."

Subsequently, this hostility persisted and gave rise to several battles and conflicts. For Muslims the issue was no less than their survival with their faith. In those circumstances, what could be the attitudes of Muslims or any other people that would have been at their place? In general all people, nations, etc. in such a situation would have fought to defend themselves.

This is precisely the subject and context of many verses that talk about fighting, and defending oneself. The first authorisation to fight for this was:

The Pilgrimage 22:39-40
"To those against whom war is made, permission is given (to fight), because they are wronged;- and verily, God is most powerful for their aid.

(They are) those who have been expelled from their homes in defiance of right,- for no cause except that they say, 'our Lord is God'.

Did not God check one set of people by means of another, there would surely have been pulled down monasteries, churches, synagogues, and mosques, in which the name of God is commemorated in abundant measure. God will certainly aid those who aid his (cause); for verily God is full of Strength, Exalted in Might, (able to enforce His Will)."

One should note that the arguments given in that verse for this permission to fight refer to a situation of self-defence. There are many other verses related to these circumstances, such as:

The Cow 2:190
"Fight in the cause of God those who fight you, but do not commit aggression ; for God does not love the transgressors."

Even in conflict situations, the Quran calls on the relevant parties for their settlement and the return to peace:
The spoils of war 8:61

"And if they incline towards peace, then incline towards it too."

The Private Apartments 49:9
"If two parties among the Believers fall into a quarrel, make peace between them."

Similar verses are in general related to these specific situations. It is of course possible to select those verses and to construct argumentations that would legitimize acts of violence and serve some purpose.

Some authors have tried to draw a general line of thought out of the previous contexts. Some of them used the fact that early verses have been abrogated: but assertions like *"God does not love the transgressors [or aggressors]" (2:190), "for God does not love those who do mischief"* (28:77), can never be a subject of abrogation.

The word "mischief" is to be understood in a broad sense that includes harming the others, making destruction in the land, etc. So that, with only these two verses one can understand the condemnation by Islam of any kind of mischief and transgression.

Using an out of context reading of the parts of the Quran that deal with the struggle for survival of the first Muslim community and the Prophet amounts to ignoring and contradicting some of the clear and definite principles cited in the beginning of this chapter about tolerance and the call for peaceful coexistence.

This peace – at several levels – that stands as a goal in the background of the Text and to which it is explicitly referred to in many places:

She to be Examined 60:8
"God does not forbid you to deal kindly and justly with those who

do not fight you for (your) Faith nor drive you out of your homes ; for God loves those who are just."

The Table 5:15-16

"There has come to you from God a (new) light and a perspicuous Book, -Wherewith God guides all who seek His good pleasure to ways of peace and safety."

6 Hadith and Sunnah - Prophet sayings and tradition

Hadiths are the collection of the sayings of the Prophet, which may be announcements, answers to questions, or dialogues about subjects related to moral, worship, daily life, etc. By extension, the Sunnah or traditions of the Prophet (literally, a well-trodden path) includes also reports about deeds and behaviour of the Prophet.

Hadiths are classified in three categories: the authentic or verified (sahih), the good (hassan) or the weak (da'if). Hadiths and Sunnah were extensively studied since the death of the Prophet with works regarding their collection, classifications and deduction of teachings. This has flourished to a branch of Islamic studies, the science of hadith.

There are several compilations of hadiths such as: Al Mouattaa (Imam Malik), Al Bukhari, Muslim, Tirmidi, Ibn Maja, etc. The assessment of the authenticity of the hadiths included in these compilations has been the subject of extensive studies, among them those of M. Albani.

The authentic hadiths and sunnah form a highly valuable source of Islamic teachings that gives useful supplements to the Quran ;

it is the second source of jurisprudence, secondary to the Quran. Here are some examples of Hadiths :

About Islam basis

"Islam has been built on five [pillars]: testifying that there is no deity worthy of worship except God and that Muhammad is the Messenger of God, establishing the Salah (prayer), paying the zakat (obligatory charity), fasting in Ramadhan and making the hajj (pilgrimage) to the House for those capable of doing so." [Agreed upon].

Love of each other

"None of you [truly] believes until he loves for his brother that which he loves for himself." [Bukhari & Muslim]

Intentions

"Actions are (judged) by motives (or intentions niyyah), so each man will have what he intended. Thus, he whose migration (hijrah) was to God and His Messenger, his migration is to God and His Messenger; but he whose migration was for some worldly thing he might gain, or for a wife he might marry, his migration is to that for which he migrated. [Bukhari & Muslim]"

Good words, communication

"Let him who believes in God and the Last Day speak good, or keep silent; and let him who believes in God and the Last Day be generous to his neighbour; and let him who believes in God and the Last Day be generous to his guest." [Bukhari & Muslim]

Charity

"Wealth does not diminish by giving Sadaqah (charity). God augments the honour of one who forgives; and one who serves another seeking the pleasure of God, God will exalt him in ranks." [Reported by Muslim]

Mercy
"The Compassionate One has mercy on those who are merciful. If you show mercy to those who are on the earth, He Who is in the heaven will show mercy to you." [Reported by Al Tirmidi]

Fasting
"Fasting is a shield." [Reported by Ahmed, Al Nassaii and Ibn Maja]
(means a protection towards many wrong actions, behaviours etc. Also a physical protection of the body)

Repentance benefits
"If anyone constantly seeks pardon (from God), God will appoint for him a way out of every distress and a relief from every anxiety, and will provide sustenance for him from where he expects not."

An advice of the Prophet
This is a reported advice of the Prophet to to Muad Ibn-Jabal:
"Be righteous (fear God) wherever you may be, and follow up a bad deed with a good deed which will wipe it out, and behave well towards the people" [Reported by Al Tirmidi]
Good deeds
"Do not consider any act of goodness as being insignificant even if it is meeting your brother with a cheerful face." [Reported by Muslim]

"Verily God has written down the good deeds and the evil deeds, and then explained it [by saying]: "Whosoever intended to perform a good deed, but did not do it, then God writes it down with Himself as a complete good deed. And if he intended to perform it and then did perform it, then God writes it down with Himself as from ten good deeds up to seven hundred times, up to many times multiplied. And if he intended to perform an evil deed, but did not do it, then God writes it down with Himself as a complete good deed. And if he intended it [i.e., the evil deed] and then performed it, then God writes it down as one evil deed." [Al-Bukhari & Muslim].

Prohibition of the reprimanded actions and change of evil

"Whosoever of you sees an evil, let him change it with his hand; and if he is not able to do so, then [let him change it] with his tongue; and if he is not able to do so, then with his heart — and that is the weakest of faith." [Reported by Muslim]

Legacy of a man

When a man dies, his deeds come to an end except for three things: Sadaqah Jariyah (ceaseless charity); a knowledge which is beneficial, or a virtuous descendant who prays for him (for the deceased)." [Reported by Muslim]

7 Selected Topics

1. The Concept of Taqwa : Piety, God-Consciousness, God-Mindfulness, ...

"Taqwa" is the Arabic term usually translated by terms like Piety, God-Consciousness, righteousness, etc. It is a central concept in the Quran that deserves some explanations, for it is simply the whole quality required from men; and what makes the distinction between them in the sight of God is not the ethnic origin, not the social standing, not the wealth, not the position in the society, but the degree of fulfilment to this quality (in the following verse, translated by 'the most righteous') :

The Apartments 49:13
*"O mankind! We created you from a male and a female, and made you into nations and tribes, that you may know each other. Verily the most honoured of you in the sight of God is **the most righteous of you**. And God is All-Knowing, All-Aware."*

We shall see that this quality encompasses all the previous prescriptions concerning good moral and good deeds as well as worship prescriptions. That is why it is considered in the Quran as a cardinal commandment given also to the People of the Book, expression that denotes those who received a revelation from God before Islam, namely Judaism and Christianity (in the following verse translated by 'to fear God'):

Women 4:131

"To God belong all things in the heavens and on earth. Verily we **have directed the People of the Book before you, and you to fear God.** *But if you deny Him, lo! unto God belong all things in the heavens and on earth, and God is Self-sufficient, worthy of all praise."*

In this short paragraph we shall talk about the issue of its translation and what does this concept precisely mean:

Literal meaning of "Taqwa": In Arabic several terms are derived from the root t.q.w. : 'Taqwa' (the quality), 'waqa' or 'Itaqa' the verbs, and 'Muttaqi' the name of who has this quality.

Literally 'Taqwa' for Man means to protect oneself from something he fears and to set oneself in a safe position regarding things that may hurt him.

In the context of Quran and Islam, 'taqwa' is specifically used to signify that one has to protect himself from potentially bad consequences when doing some actions or having some behaviours or when not performing some duties. These duties and moral rules are those prescribed by God; that is why in the translations we find expressions like :

- Those who do their duties : T. Ivring's translation
- God-Consciousness, Those who are God-conscious: In Muhammad Asad's translation.
- God-mindfulness, Those who are God-mindful: In Abdel Haleem and M.W. Khan translations.
- Piety: in many other translations (French, etc.)
- Those who fear God, or who are righteous, depending on verses : Yusuf Ali's translation
- The fearing and obeying (Mohamad Ahmad and Samira

Ahmad dictionary and literal translation of the Quran)
- Those who protect or guard themselves : in J.Berque's French translation

When reading the Quran we notice a frequent use of the term 'taqwa' as if it should be understood in its intuitive or literal meaning or if one has to develop his own understanding of the concept when wondering what it ought to contain through the explanation of the Quran itself.

The two possibilities seem to be valid: the first one (literal and intuitive meaning) suggests a sort of general righteousness, fulfilment of duties, repentance in case of sin or mistake, etc. with the intent to avoid consequences of disobedience (hence, according to the literal meaning, to guard oneself from bad consequences if one is to commit a bad action or a sin etc.).

As for the second one, the careful reader of the Quran will notice that it actually provides explanations and some precise conditions included in this concept of God-mindfulness:

The Cow 2:1-5
"*A.L.M. This is the Book in which there is no doubt, a guidance for those who are mindful of God;*
Who believe in the Unseen, are steadfast in prayer, and spend out of what We have provided for them;
And who believe in the Revelation sent to you, and sent before your time, and are certain of the Hereafter.
They are on true guidance from their Lord, and these will be the successful."

The Cow 2:177
"Goodness is not *that you turn your faces towards east or west;* *but goodness is to believe in God and the Last Day, and the*

Angels, and the Book, and the Messengers;
to spend of your substance, out of love for Him, for your relatives,
for orphans, for the needy, for the wayfarer, for those who ask,
and for the ransom of slaves;
to be steadfast in prayer, and practice regular charity;
to fulfil the promise when you have made one ;
and to be firm and patient, in pain and adversity, and in times of
danger. ***Such are the people of truth, the God-fearing.****"*

The Family of Imran 3:133-134
"Be quick in the race for forgiveness from your Lord, and for a
Garden whose width is that of the whole of the heavens and of the
*earth, prepared **for the righteous [the God-mindful the God-***
fearing],
Those who spend freely, whether in prosperity, or in adversity;
who restrain anger, and pardon people ; for God loves the doers
of good;
And those who, when they commit a shameful deed, or wronged
their own souls, earnestly bring God to mind, and ask for
forgiveness for their sins,- and who can forgive sins except God?-
and are never obstinate in persisting knowingly in the wrong they
have done.
For such the reward is forgiveness from their Lord, and Gardens
with rivers flowing underneath,- an eternal dwelling: How
excellent a recompense for those who work and strive!"

We deduce from these verses some qualities and conditions that compose the concept of God-mindfulness: to accomplish prayer, to spend for the needy, to believe in this revelation and the former ones (reference to the books revealed), to fulfil one's engagements, to observe patience, to do good deeds, to show restraint when you are angry, to pardon those who offend you, to repent of your sins and ask forgiveness whenever you commit a shameful deed or having sinned against yourself.

This God-mindfulness or righteousness summarizes therefore the qualities advocated by Islam to which the believer has to conform to by doing his best, first by acquiring the high moral standards, understanding the motivations, being aware of his deeds, learning from his experience, his mistakes and that of the others; the mistakes or sins can hardly be completely avoided, this quest of righteousness is thus a way of continuous improvement for the lifetime.

We mention at this stage this saying of the Prophet advising one of his companions, Muad Ibn-Jabal:

"Be righteous (fear God) wherever you may be, and follow up a bad deed with a good deed which will wipe it out, and behave well towards the people"

2. Unity of God and non-association of partners to Him

The first and fundamental principle of Islam, which is greatly emphasized in the Quran, is the belief in God, one and only one, the Creator, Sustainer of the universe and all the creatures therein. All kinds of association of other partner to God are vigorously rejected and considered as a major sin.

Women 4:36
"Worship God, and associate nothing with Him"

The Night Journey 17:22
" Do not set up with God another god ; lest you will sit in disgrace and destitution."

Sign spelled out 41:6
"Say : 'I am but a human being like you: It is revealed to me, that your God is one God'."

90

In the beginning of the 2d Surah we note this emphasis on non-association preceded by a basic argumentation:

The Cow 2:21-22
O you people! Worship your Lord, who created you and those who came before you, so that you may become righteous;
Who has made the earth your couch, and the heavens your canopy; and sent down rain from the heavens; and brought forth therewith Fruits for your sustenance; ***then do not set up rivals unto God when you know (the truth).***

The Cow 2:165
"Yet there are men who take others besides God, as equal with Him: They love them as they should love God. But those of Faith are overflowing in their love for God. If only the unrighteous could see, behold, they would see the torment ; that to God belongs all power, and God is severe in punishment.
Then those who were followed clear themselves of those who followed them ; They would see the torment, and all ties between them would be cut off. "

Jonah 10:106
"Nor call on any, other than God ; Such will neither profit you nor hurt you. If you do, behold! you shall certainly be of the wrong doers."

Kneeling 45:23
"Have you seen the one who has taken his own vain desire as his god?"

Although, the concept of non-association is so important, it does not seem to be fully apprehended in all its dimensions, which, as we shall see, requires reflection about the numerous verses related to it with their implications, motivations and context of applications. As a result we witness several beliefs, attitudes and practices that fit indeed within the scope of the 'association of partner(s) to God', not only throughout history but also in our present societies. Also, the scholars use to distinguish between the 'big association' sin and the small one.

1ˢᵗ aspect of Unity of God and non-association:

The first side lays in the idolatry belief of ancient civilisations when people took certain objects as divinity, like the sun, the moon, Icons, etc. Sometimes these people may believe in God but ascribe to Him idols as partners, which become main objects of worship, as it was the case in the pre-islamic Arabia. These kinds of beliefs have not completely disappeared in the present time.

2d aspect:

In some cases Prophets may be so venerated that they become associated to God in worship or that they are attributed divine qualities or power, a trend about which the Quran issues warning at many occasions:

The Family of Imran : 3:79-80
"It is not possible that a man, to whom is given the Book, and Wisdom, and the prophetic office, say to people: "Be ye my worshippers rather than God's": on the contrary He would say "Be faithful worshippers of your Lord : For you have taught the Book and you have studied it earnestly."
Nor would he instruct you to take angels and prophets for Lords and patrons. What! would he bid you to unbelief [denial] after you have submitted to God ?"

3d aspect:

The previous side of the association is greatly emphasized in the case of Jesus Christ, considered in the Quran as a highly privileged Prophet:

The family of Imran 3:45
"Behold! the angels said: "O Mary! God gives you glad tidings of a Word from Him: his name will be the Christ, Jesus the son of Mary, held in honour in this world and the Hereafter and of the company of those nearest to God."

However Islam strongly refutes any divine quality attributed to Jesus as well as that of being the son of God or a partner in Lordship:

The family of Imran 3:64
"Say: 'O People of the Book! come to common terms as between us and you: That we worship none but God; that we associate no partners with Him; that we do not take, from among ourselves, Lords and patrons other than God.' If then they turn back, then say : 'Bear witness that we at least are submitted to God's Will'."

The Table 5:75
"The Messiah, son of Mary was no more than a Messenger; many were the Messengers that passed away before him. His mother was a woman of truth. They had both to eat their (daily) food."

Women 4:171
"O People of the Book! Commit no excesses in your religion ; Nor say of God aught but the truth. (The Messiah) Christ Jesus, the son of Mary was only Messenger of God, and His Word, which He bestowed on Mary, and a spirit proceeding from Him: so believe in God and His Messengers."

4th aspect:

Actually, the Quran considers that the unity of God is both a basic principle of faith and a fact that could be argued by its necessity character for the integrity of the Creation and its continuation:

The Prophets 21:22
"If there were, in the heavens and the earth, other gods besides God, then both would have gone to ruin ! but glory to God, the Lord of the Throne. High is He above what they attribute to Him." (in Ivring translation: *"they (heavens and earth) would both dissolve in chaos"*)

The Believers 23:91
"No son did God beget, nor is there any god along with Him: if there were many gods, behold, each god would have taken away what he had created, and some would have lorded it over others! Glorified be God above all that they allege"

That is why Man is urged to express all the praise to God specifically about this unity, in having one God, All-wise and All-knowing, the Sustainer of the Creation who insures its integrity and is in charge of its destiny:

The Night Journey 17:111
"And say, 'Praise be to God, who begets no son, and has no partner in sovereignty, nor needs He any to protect Him from weakness', and magnify Him for His greatness and glory."

5th aspect:

This proscription of ascribing any divine partnership to God when it is about showing a cult to Prophets or saints is obviously valid for any other cult of personality for someone dead or alive.

The Night Journey 17:56-57
"Say: 'Call on those - besides Him - whom you fancy: they have neither the power to remove your troubles from you nor to change them.'
Those whom they call upon do desire (for themselves) means of access to their Lord, - whoever of them is nearest - : they hope for

His Mercy and fear His Wrath; for the Wrath of your Lord is to be feared."

The Thunder 13:16
"Say: 'Who is the Lord and Sustainer of the heavens and the earth?' Say: 'It is God.' Say: 'Do you then take protectors other than Him, such as have no power either for good or for harm to themselves?' Say: 'Are the blind equal with those who see? Or the depths of darkness equal with light?' Or do they assign to God partners who have created anything as He has created, so that the creation seemed to them similar? Say: 'God is the Creator of all things ; He is the One, the Supreme and Irresistible.'"

6th aspect:

Also, this strong requirement of non-association of any partner to God is not merely a matter of belief and intellectual position. In fact, in some situations Man may be facing concrete choices or actions which would express the extent of his loyalty to this belief.

To illustrate this in simple words: Your manager / commander or chief officer asks you to perform or (to take) some immoral action (decision), such as making an unfair judgement, or an act of corruption or a harmful action towards someone, etc. Your job, position or career relies on your loyalty to and good relation with your chief.

So that you have to choose between, on one hand obedience to your chief and maintaining (or increasing) the privileges you have and on the other hand the obedience to God by respecting the moral values prescribed; in the later case you feel that you may lose your job, your position which will undermine your material conditions with all the consequences this may have; this is the appearance of that situation.

The first choice is an example of attributing a partner to God where one fears this partner and expecting rewards from him more than he does from God ; this is an erroneous idea on the relation one should have with God : the true believer considers that all what he has is a gift from God:

The Bee 16:53
"Whatever blessing you enjoy is from God. And when you are touched by distress, unto Him you cry with groans;"

The second choice, which is apparently risky, expresses the faithfulness to God and His Unity, attitude where the ethics are placed above material considerations. Man may face in his lifetime this kind of situations, where his conscience is in test and sometimes this leads to tough choices.

This is exemplified in the Quran (as it is the case for Judaism and Christianity) by the Prophet Abraham whose obedience to God in extremely difficult situations makes him, a model (Imam) for believers according to the Quran, symbolizing the loyalty to God and His Unity

The Cow 2:124
"And remember that Abraham was tried by his Lord with certain commands, which he fulfilled ; He said: 'I will make thee an Imam (A model, a leader) to the people'."

The Bees 16:120-123
"Abraham was indeed a model, devoutly obedient to God, and true in Faith, and was not of those who ascribe divinity to aught beside God.
He showed his gratitude for the favours of God, Who chose him, and guided him to a Straight Way.
And We gave him Good in this world, and he will be, in the Hereafter, in the ranks of the Righteous.
So We have revealed to you: 'Follow the ways of Abraham who

was the True in Faith, and was not of those who ascribe divinity to aught beside God'."

To conclude:

The reader of the Quran will notice the repeated reference to this imperative of non-attributing any partner to God; this emphasis occurs within several contexts most likely in order to show all the dimensions of this requirement. The previous cases aim at presenting some of these implications, noting that the subject deserves a more elaborate study. The true adoption of the principle of unity of God goes far beyond a simple belief but leads to requirements in one's lifetime that concern the sincerity of the faith and that may condition some decisive choices when Man has to express that his values are prior to other considerations.

3. The last Surah of the Quran : Man and God's help against evil in time of whispers

The last surah (in the Text and not chronological order) entitled *Mankind* or *People* is:

"Say: I seek refuge with the Lord of Mankind,
The King of Mankind,
The God of Mankind,-
From the mischief of the whisperer of evil, who withdraws after his whisper,-
The same who whispers into the hearts of Mankind,-
Among Jinns and among men"

We shall make here an attempt of interpretation of this surah, which shows that its content is rather deep and contrasts with its concise character.

It is about the whisperer with its disturbance and bad influence on Man by inciting him to evil thoughts and actions and man is called on to ask or pray God for help in order to deliver him from this harmful influence especially when with his will, his capabilities, he is not able to overcome the bad temptations of evil.

It is a fact that the evil is an issue for Man since the dawn of humanity. It is of course not just a philosophical topic but a real problem at social and political levels, with a broad range in its manifestation: from bad thoughts, bad words to all reprimanded actions: theft, corruption, adultery, individual crimes, organized crimes, etc.

Acts of evil could originate from passions and desires of man:

The Criterion 25:43

"Have you seen the *one who has taken for his god his own passion ? Could you be a protecter over him?*"

On the other hand the surah 'Mankind' refers eventually to forces that can influence men, misguide them, making an evil action seemingly a righteous one. The existence of creatures like the devil whose work is to deceive men and to orient them to mistakes, evil and sins, is part of the facts mentioned in the Quran:

The Ants 27:24

"*... Satan has made their deeds seem pleasing in their eyes, and has kept them away from the Path.*"

However, at this stage we can just admit that when Man is in a position to commit an evil action, he may have the feeling that this step is not rightful but he does have the opposite feeling that this action is a good thing to do for what it will bring; this incitement to the evil action is somewhat hidden in that man thinks or considers the idea as his; whence the indication *"From the mischief of the whisperer of evil, who withdraws after his whisper"* (Trans. Of Y. Ali) or *"from the evil of the stealthy whisperer"* (Trans. Of T. Irving).

But when Man succumbs to the temptation, he becomes responsible of his action whatever the source of the idea is, and he and the society will face the consequences of this and all the bad actions which occur in our world.

Hence the surah 'Mankind' urges Man to stand cautious and lucid when he doubts about the rightfulness of an action that does not seem compatible with his values.

And when he feels overwhelmed by temptation, the Quran through this surah calls on him to ask or pray for the support of God who is the All-knowing, All-powerful, who perfectly knows one's case, one's thoughts, one's intent, and one's weakness.

This appeal to God is therefore an act of worship which has a decisive purpose, that is to not take wrong steps that are harmful to Man and his society: evil actions cannot lead to anything other than sorrow, sadness, and sometimes disasters.

Other purpose:
The surah 114 is also relevant in some cases well-known to psychologists: that is when Man is subject to very bad whispers, mind disturbance suggesting to him extreme, even foolish ideas: insulting others (including family), illusions, ideas of suicide, etc.

Along his lifetime Man hears many bad expressions and sees many bad behaviours and ideas. All these remain registered in his mind; in certain occasions (anger, conflict, drugs or alcohol effect, euphoria, or a pathologic state of mind), these ideas come back to mind being naively considered as good ones to reflect upon, to say or to do. These thoughts may be so extravagant that Man has doubts about himself wondering whether he is becoming crazy.

The Quran tells us that these thoughts may be the results of a devil whispers (and other influential factors): this whisperer is stealthy and hidden in the sense that Man considers that all these ideas are his ; besides the surah 114, there are many mentions about this devil role:

The Cow 2:275
" ... *whom the evil one by his touch has driven to madness.* "

Women 4:60
"... *But Satan's wish is to lead them astray far away from the right.*"

When facing such a situation, one has to be aware that:
-first, these bad thoughts and ideas are not necessarily his, but are eventually from external whisperers; in considering this Man has no longer this feeling of guilt and this puts him in a position to face the bad intentions rather than asking questions about himself.

-second, not paying much attentions to theses 'noises' and matching ideas with the reason, the good sense, the ethical values. All thoughts and ideas that are manifestly harmful and non-compatible with one's values are to be considered as irrelevant and may be devil's promptings trying to deceive him and puts him into troubles.

-third, to be cautious when one is thinking about negative ideas, for instance those inspiring him that his situation is very bad, etc. The simple repetition of these negative thoughts, lead to the belief that this is true and that the situation is actually very bad (which is not really the case if one makes calmly a fair assessment), which would make the perception worse, and may lead to anxious or depressive states.

-fourth, if at last, this use of one's reasoning and will is not sufficient to pass this episode of bad temptations, - which might be possible in certain cases, and that is why we witness these kind of situations - then Man is urged to request help from the Almighty God. In addition to the 'Mankind' surah, there are many references in the Quran to these situations:

The Heights 7:200-201
"If a suggestion from Satan assail your mind, seek refuge with God; for He is All-Hearing and All-Knowing.
Those who fear God, when a thought of evil from Satan assaults them, bring God to remembrance, when lo! they see aright !"

The Believers 23:97-98
"And say 'O my Lord! I seek refuge with You from the suggestions of the evil ones.
And I seek refuge with You O my Lord! So that they may not come near me'."

As a conclusion:
The surah N°114 has both a first practical side concerning the endeavour that man ought to have for the good and against the evil and a second side concerning a link between this evil and some of its sources; namely, besides the passions and impulses of man himself, the devil(s) origin of this incitement; a fact that goes back to the episode of the Creation of man cf. The Cow 2:29-38 and The Heights 7:10-29. And by this we have a link with the very purpose of life according to the Quran *"He Who created Death and Life, that He may try which of you is best in deed"*

(The Sovereignty 67:2).

Along the history, Man has struggled against evil phenomena and has built up organizations, legal instruments and others that implement some ethical corpus: from the education systems which have both vocational and educational goals to legal systems, security arsenal, and international organizations which aims at addressing important human issues in a fairly evolved way, etc.

Despite the huge progress of humanity and the increasing consciousness about the responsibility of Man in sustaining a peaceful existence, our societies are still subject to numerous acts (individual crimes, qualified as isolated, organized crimes, wars and conflicts) harming the hoped peaceful life at all levels : individual, family to international level. Furthermore, one may have the impression that these phenomena are likely to continue their occurrence until the end of the times.

Our societies, being formed by individuals with various backgrounds, whose thoughts and behaviours are subject to several influential factors, all their actions begin first in their minds. Good education is of course the first lever of action of any society in order to prevent harmful ideas and actions. But it is far from being sufficient.

This surah closes the Quran by reminding men that they ultimately ought to rely on God's support in order to deliver them (in fact, their mind) from the evil and bad temptations, for the good of their lives here and the hereafter:

The Cow 2:38
"... *there comes to you Guidance from Me, whosoever follows My guidance, on them shall be no fear, nor shall they grieve.*"

8 The Quran: Style, Structure and content

1. The status of the Quran

For Islam, the Quran is the book revealed by God to the Prophet Muhammad. This revelation was spread over twenty three years (~610 to 632). The Quran is considered as the authentic word of God and not an inspired text. The Quran gives itself a remark on this status at its very beginning, just after the Opening surah:

The Cow 2:2
"A.L.M. This is the Book; in which there is no doubt, a guidance for those who are mindful of God"

There is no Arabic text that has similarities with the Quran in the style, the content or the structure. Some attempts which aimed at producing fragments of text or wording similar to the Quran had been made, but to no avail.

The Cow 2:23
"And if you are in doubt as to what We have revealed to Our servant, then produce a Sura like thereunto; and call your witnesses or helpers besides God if your are truthful. And if you cannot do this - and you never will - ..."

The verse 2:2 may also be understood with regard to Quran's content: It is a text of all the times, all people, all societies and cultures, and when being read by a person it is a book intended for all ages, and whatever the experience, the maturity one has, he will find relevant messages of guidance for him. At the same time it is indicated in the Quran that some parts or verses required specific background and one has to ask the scholars for the true meanings.

The Quran is also a sacred book:

The Inevitable 56:77-81
"That this is indeed a Quran most honourable,
In Book well-guarded,
Which none shall touch but those who are clean:
A Revelation from the Lord of the Worlds.
Is it this Statement that you scorn, ?"

The way this revelation of God to the Prophet Muhammed had occurred does not trouble or raise a problem for believers, for whom God, Who has power over everything, can pass on messages by various means. The Quran and the tradition mention that this revelation had happened through the Angel Gabriel.

2. Structure and style of the Quran

The Quran consists of 114 chapters and the surahs are often classified according to their length. The longest ones are in general at the beginning of the Text. Each surah is formed of numbered verses.

Names of the Suras
The surahs bear names deriving from a subject or an event dealt with. For instance:
-Surah 2, The Cow (al-Baqara): its name is likely related to the episode where Moses asks the Hebrews to sacrifice a cow.

-Surah 3, The Family of Imran (Al-Imran) and Surah 19, Mary (Myriam): their names are related to Jesus Christ, one of the topics treated.

-Surah 5, The Table (al-Maida): its name relates to a scene which happened between Jesus Christ and the Apostles.

The Chapters are both independent and interdependent

It is not necessary to read a given Surah in order to read another one. At the same time a subject dealt with in a given Surah may be further explained or completed in other places of the Quran.

Arrangement of the Text

The Quran is not arranged in chronological order: the actual order of the verses does not follow :

– the chronology of revelation: the first verses revealed are those of the surahs 96, whereas the last one (or one of the last ones) is the verse 281 of the surah 2.

– nor the chronology of events reported: the events are not mentioned in chronological order since the creation.

The chapters and verses of the Quran are themselves not arranged in thematic order: a subject (for example: the creation, charity, prayer) is dealt with in many places of the text.

A careful reading of a Surah brings to the fore a structure of one or several themes and a global coherence stands out despite the apparent interlacing of the subjects. The explanations regarding the structure of the chapters have given rise to many studies.

Repetition of subjects in the Quran: some important motivations

We shall confine ourselves here to give some quick remarks about this:

– The repetition of themes is not merely a literary device but may have an educational purpose, especially when the subjects are treated from different angles ;

- Indeed, men do need continuous reminders about some subjects: our daily occupations, with busy schedules (or not) put man in a situation of forgetting some important aspects of our life, our duties and we can even make mistakes in setting our priorities. It turns out that these important sides of life, these duties, the actions that should matter for everyone, are precisely among the main subjects of the Quran : some actions like charity, spending for the needy, remembrance of God, and attitudes in the daily life: being fair, telling good words, forgiveness, etc. and all these topics can be found in various places of the Quran from its beginning to the end. Hence by regular reading, one will find important guidance at many places of the text which constitute therefore a reminder to Man. the Quran also qualified itself by the term 'Dhikr' which corresponds, among other meanings, to the verb 'remind'. Repeating important subjects in various situations and places is a highly relevant way to convey a message, from an educational point a view.

- On the other hand this enables the reader of a given part of the Text to find many instructive ideas and messages, without being obliged to read the full Text : repetition of the above mentioned important topics is of course necessary for this feature.

- This redundancy is also a call for a synthesis ability and reflection: namely, to not have a final and definitive idea until all the elements on the subject are treated in different contexts.

- The revelation circumstances and its spreading over more than twenty years, and the fact that the Prophet came across extremely difficult situations, with regard to the persecutions coming from those who reject this revelation, the hypocrites, etc.; the Quran has then reported regularly examples of previous Prophets and the difficulties they encountered, as an example:

Noah 71: 1-7
"1 We sent Noah to his People (with the Command): "warn your People before there comes to them a painful retribution."
2 He said: "O my People! I am to you a Warner, clear and open:
3 "That you should worship God, fear Him and obey me:
4 "So He may forgive you your sins and give you respite for a stated Term ; for when the   Term given by God is accomplished, it cannot be put forward if you only knew."
5 He said: "O my Lord! I have called to my People night and day,
6 "But my call only increases their flight from the Right.
7 "And every time I have called to them, that You might forgive them, they have only thrust their fingers into their ears, covered themselves up with their garments, grown obstinate, and given themselves up to arrogance""

In the following verses, it is said that the remembrance of the experience of ancient people and Prophets aims, among other purposes, at giving moral support to the Prophet Muhammad in his struggle for making a place to the faith he was proclaiming:

Hud 11:120
"All that We relate to You of the stories of the Messengers,- with it We make firm your heart: in them there comes to you the Truth, as well as an exhortation and a message of remembrance to those who believe."

The criterion 25:32
"Those who reject Faith say: "Why is not the Qur'an revealed to him all at once? Thus is it revealed, that We may strengthen your heart thereby, and We have rehearsed it to you in slow, well-arranged stages, gradually""

Also some prescriptions were announced gradually. It is the case, for example, of the prohibition of alcohol and gambling which are treated several times in The Quran.

The Cow 2:219
"They ask you concerning wine and gambling. Say: "In them is great sin, and some profit, for men; but the sin is greater than the profit."

The Table 5:90:
"O you who believe! Wine and gambling, dedication of stones, and divination by arrows, are an abomination,- of Satan's handwork : so avoid them, that you may succeed."

The Quran style

The Quran style is unique in its elegance, conciseness, expression mode and eloquence. As an example, the Surah Joseph, reports facts essentially similar to the corresponding story of the Old Testament, but in a very distinguished style which is furthermore marked by the statement of rules and wisdom to be drawn at several stages of the story, which makes the narrative so admirable. At the end, the Surah points out the goals, with an important conclusion :

Joseph 12:111
There is, in their stories, instruction for men endued with understanding. It is not a tale invented, but a confirmation of what went before it,- a detailed exposition of all things, and a guide and a mercy to those who believe.

In addition to the previous remarks regarding chronological and thematic order, let us mention that the Quran shows a very contrasted alternation in type and intensity of exhortation, messages of reminder, warning and hope:

– For instance, a message of warning :

The pilgrimage 22:1-4:
"O mankind! fear your Lord! for the convulsion of the Hour of Judgement is a tremendous thing !

The Day you shall see it, every mother giving suck shall forget her suckling-babe, and every pregnant female shall drop her load unformed ; you shall see mankind as in a drunken riot, yet not drunk ; but dreadful will be the Wrath of God."

A message of serenity :

Taha 20:1-4
"Ta-Ha. We have not sent down the Qur'an to cause you any hardship,
But only as a reminder to those who fear (God),
A revelation from Him Who created the earth and the hight heavens."

A verse containing both a warning and hope for forgiveness:

The Table 5:98
" You should know that God is severe in punishment and that God is Most Forgiving, Most Merciful."

A message of hope towards sinners :

The Groups 39:53:
"Say: "O my Servants who have transgressed against their souls! Do not despair of the Mercy of God: for God forgives all sins: for He is Most Forgiving, Most Merciful."

An alternation in the subjects:
Transition from serious situations to practical details, like for

instance, in the Surah 2 where there is a transition from the verse 281 on death to a verse on practical prescriptions dealing with debt:

The Cow 2:281:
"And fear the Day when you will be brought back to God. Then shall every soul be paid what it earned, and no one will be wronged."

Transition from indications regarding customs to the famous verse giving men an idea about the reality of God:

The Light 24:33
"Let those who do not find the wherewithal for marriage keep themselves chaste, until God gives them means out of His grace."

Light 24:35
"God is the Light of the heavens and the earth. The Parable of His Light is as if there were a Niche and within it a Lamp: the Lamp enclosed in Glass: the glass is like a brilliant star: Lit from a blessed Tree, an Olive, neither of the east nor of the west, whose oil would almost illuminate, though fire has not touched it: Light upon Light! God guides whom He wills to His Light: God sets forth Parables for men: and God is Knower of all things."

At a first reading, the reader non familiar with the Quran will notice a succession of topics and transitions, but a more careful study will lead to a better understanding of the meaning and the order of the verses. The use of exegesis works can be useful in this respect. Here is another example:

The sequence of the verses The Cow 2:226-242 is dealing with family issues that sometimes turn to be serious ones, and suddenly in the verses 238-239 there is a transition to another topic, the prayer and a reminder urging believers to hold it regularly:

110

The Cow 2:238

"Take care over doing your prayers, including the Middle Prayer; and stand before God in devotion."

The text returns back, after these two verses, to the initial topic of family issues. At a first sight one may not understand this double transition or the links with the two subjects. There may be several reasons of this as it is certainly the case for the positions of every verse in the text.

The following interpretation is a plausible reason in the latter case: prayer is one of the most important prescription in Islam as it symbolises and insure the continuous spiritual relation between Man and God with all its consequences. It should be performed at its time. In particular, being occupied with some problem however complex and important it may be, should not distract Man from prayer. Furthermore, asking help and guidance from God in every issue is precisely one of the prayer's goals and therefore performing it at its time, not only shows that this duty is considered as it should be, but also this prayer would provide help and guidance in adopting the right approach and solution regarding the issue or problems one is concerned with. In prayer Man is supposed to retrieve his tranquillity and serenity. He is standing before the Almighty God, asking guidance and help for everything. Also, provided that prayer is performed with humility, sincerity and focus (especially by not being distracted by one's material issues), it may undoubtedly help to avoid any decision taken impulsively or in an anger context which is likely to be a wrong one. This explanation is likely to be a motivation of the transition cited above.

The Quran also indicates that it contains unequivocal verses as well as other parts which can be subjected to interpretations.

The Family of Imran 3:7

"He it is Who has sent down to thee the Book: In it are verses of established meaning ; they are the foundation of the Book ; others are allegorical. But those in whose hearts is perversity follow the part thereof that is allegorical, seeking discord, and searching for its hidden meanings, but no one knows its hidden meanings except God. And those who are firmly grounded in knowledge say: "We believe in the Book; the whole of it is from our Lord" and none will grasp the Message except men of understanding."

3. Content

The Quran addresses subjects which are essential for humans, both for helping them to get an understanding of the world we are living in and for providing guidance in all circumstances of life. Thus as previously mentioned, we find:

- A conception of the world: the creation of universe and mankind, the Creator, the purpose of existence, life, death, human being destiny, the Hereafter (the beyond, resurrection, etc.).
- Worship prescriptions: this part deals with the relationship between Man and God, His Creator : we find : the prayers and remembrance of God, Spending, charity or Alms-giving, Fasting and the pilgrimage.
- Basic moral values and principles: which have to govern human's behaviour and their relationship: Uprightness, Freedom, Solidarity, Justice, Tolerance, Forgiveness, Humility, Patience, fulfilment of commitments, advocating righteousness and preventing blameable actions, moderation, honesty, etc.
- Guidance to humans : in addition to the previous points, we mention here the appeal to learn, to develop one's knowledges, use one's reasoning capabilities, to work and do one's best to achieve good deeds.

- Some specific prescriptions which concern particular topics: Family, rights and duties of men, women, children, rules of the inheritance, few prescriptions regarding foods, etc.
- Some instances: the message of the Quran is widely illustrated by historical episodes about ancient People, in particular those who had received Divine messages: the episodes about the Hebrews occupy a great deal of the stories and instances related by the Quran. These narratives are reminded to Man with the intent to draw lessons and morals of the experience of these people.

As for the rest, the Quran calls on men for the use of reason and intelligence and all abilities whereby they have been preferred to many other creatures and which must be in the service of human material and moral progress.

Humans have indeed all the skills to establish legislations regarding life in society; these legislations are of course dependent of time, cultures, progress levels of societies, political and ideological trends, etc.

An ideology might be in fashion for a certain time but no longer in order after some decades or centuries.

However on certain fundamental subjects, there must be some principles, rules and values which provide mankind with a moral reference that is valid for all the times.

It is precisely the purpose of the Quran: the moral values quoted above (uprightness, freedom, justice, solidarity, etc.) are in fact considered in the present times as universal. The great emphasis on learning, using the reason, and all Man capabilities and skills for human progress implies in fact that the moral reference of the Quran is widely opened to human intelligence: with this, Man is in position to deal with his social, economic, or political concerns; he has a responsibility for that.

The Quran is a book of wisdom, of moral reference ; at the end of the sequences of commandments we read:

The Night Journey 17:39
"These are among the precepts of wisdom, which your Lord has revealed to you."

And the Quran talks about this wisdom as the best quality and gift one could be granted:

The Cow 2:269
"He grants wisdom to whom He pleases; and whoever is granted wisdom has indeed been granted abundant good; but none will grasp the Message but men of understanding"

The Quran has given rise to a large amount of works, studies and exegesis since the first centuries of Islam.

Further remarks on the text of Quran

- At a first reading, one should not seek to get a full understanding of all the verses and the messages conveyed.
- In fact, the reader may be rather surprised about the successions of themes through the text: some verses are clear at a first reading but others requires explanations, for instance those related to some events either in the Prophet's era or regarding ancient People (the Hebrews for example) : *it is not necessary to have a specific background for continuing the text.* Many parts are discussed in other places of the text.
- The understanding one can have of some verses or parts may evolve with time, for instance :

Gathering 64:15
"Your possessions and your children may be but a trial. Whereas with God, is the highest reward."

Iron 57:20

"You should know, that the life of this world is but play and amusement, pomp and mutual boasting and multiplying, in rivalry among yourselves, in respect of money and children.

Here is a similitude: How rain and the growth which it brings forth, delight (the hearts of) the tillers; soon it withers; you will see it grow yellow; then it becomes dry and crumbles away"

- These verses may not be understood in the same way by a person in his twenties and the same person in his sixties. This is true for many subjects: the moral values such as patience, uprightness, justice, etc. Their full scope and therefore the meanings and motivations of the related verses become clear and more evolved with Man's experience and maturity.

- That is why the Quran is intended for multiple readings. One would discover each time new ideas or interpretation: as was said by Thomas B. Ivring in the introduction of his translation of the Quran "Translation is literally impossible because interpretation in another language is an ongoing process, especially with a document that must be used constantly. Almost every day I learn a new rendering for a word or phrase; then I must run this new thread of meaning through other passages. The Quran is a living Book. We must respect yet find a way to interpret this sacred text, and not deform its meaning"

At this stage, the reader has to refer to the extracts of the Quran or to the entire text.

4. Historical notes

As was previously mentioned, the Quran was not revealed all at once, but in fragments; each time a fragment was revealed, the Prophet asked one of his companions to transcribe it by specifying the exact place of the verse in the Quran (Surah and the number of the verse).

Moreover, the Quran was learned by some Prophet's companions, and in the months of Ramadan, the whole of the Quran revealed was recited. The tradition tells us also that the Quran was recited twice during the months of Ramadan that preceded the Prophet's death.

After the Prophet's death, the Caliphs Abu Bakr and Omar worked for the gathering of the Quran parts in one single manuscript which was then confided to Hafsa, a Prophet Widow. Then, the Caliph Othman, successor of Caliph Omar, undertook to gather a compilation of the Quran. A commission of experts was appointed for that purpose, having as members Zayd Ibn Thabit - the secretary of the Prophet. This commission is supposed to have used all the existing manuscripts with the help of the companions who had totally or partially learned the Quran.

So, a rigorous work was done to gather the text of the Quran. The compilation gathered in this way was supposed to coincide with the manuscript of Hafsa. Several copies of this Text were transcribed and sent out to some of the big cities of the emerging Islamic regions.

The Quran has the original feature that it can be utterly learned without much difficulty both in adulthood and childhood. In the Islamic countries, there are many children in traditional pre-school and schools who learned the Quran entirely around the age of 10 and recited it at this young age without making an error.

This fact (learning easily the Quran) as well as the involvement of the Prophet's companions who knew the Quran two years after the end of revelation (for the Hafsa manuscript) and a dozen of years for Othman's compilation enables to assert beyond doubt the authenticity of the Text. Besides, a believer is inclined to think that given the huge importance of the Text, which is the literal word of God, He will make its compilation possible and without any alteration; the Quran itself brings up this fact:

The Resurrection 75:16-19:
"Surely, upon Us rests its safe collection and its recital.
.. and upon Us rests its clear explanation."

Rock City 15: 9
"Verily, We have sent down the Reminder*; and We will assuredly guard it."
(*) Means The Quran.

Part II : Selected Extracts from the Quran

Selected Extracts from the Quran

1. God

The Cow 2:255

God! There is no god but He,-the Living, the Self-subsisting, The Sustainer. No slumber can seize Him nor sleep. His are all things in the heavens and on earth. Who is there can intercede in His presence except with His permission? He knows what is before them and what is behind them. They can not compass aught of His knowledge except as He wills. His Throne extends over the heavens and the earth, and and He is never weary of preserving them for He is the Most High, the Great.

Light 24:35

God is the Light of the heavens and the earth. The Parable of His Light is as if there were a Niche and within it a Lamp ; the Lamp enclosed in Glass ; the glass is like a brilliant star ; Lit from a blessed Tree, an Olive, neither of the east nor of the west, whose oil would almost illuminate, though fire has not touched it; Light upon Light! God guides whom He wills to His Light. God sets forth Parables for men; and God is Knower of all things.

Exile 59:22-24

He is God, than Whom there is no other god; -Who knows all things both secret and open; He, Most Gracious, Most Merciful.

He is God, than Whom there is no other god;- the Sovereign, the Holy One, the Source of Peace, the Granter of security, the Supreme, the Almighty, the Most Powerful, the Most Dignified. Glory to God! (High is He) above the partners they attribute to Him.

He is God, the Creator, the Initiator, the Designer. To Him belong the Most Beautiful Names; whatever is in the heavens and on earth, do declare His Praises and Glory, and He is the Exalted in Might, the Wise.

Iron 57:1-6

Whatever is in the heavens and on earth,- let it declare the Praises and Glory of God; for He is the Exalted in Might, the Wise.

To Him belongs the dominion of the heavens and the earth; It is He Who gives Life and Death; and He has Power over all things.

He is the First and the Last, the Evident and the Immanent; and He has full knowledge of all things.

He is Who created the heavens and the earth in Six Days, and is moreover firmly established on the Throne of Authority. He knows what enters within the earth and what comes forth out of it, what comes down from heaven and what mounts up to it.

And He is with you wheresoever you may be. And God sees well all that you do.

To Him belongs the dominion of the heavens and the earth, and all affairs are referred back to God.
He merges Night into Day, and He merges Day into Night; and He has full knowledge of the secrets of all hearts.

The Romans 30:17- 19

So Glory to God, when you reach evening and when you rise in the morning;

And to Him be praise, in the heavens and on earth; and in the late afternoon and when you are at your midday.

It is He Who brings out the living from the dead, and brings out the dead from the living, and Who gives life to the earth after it is dead, and thus shall you be brought out (from the dead).

The Heights 7:143-144

When Moses came to the place appointed by Us, and his Lord addressed him, He said: "O my Lord! show Yourself to me, that I may look upon You." God said: "You will not see Me ; But look upon the mount; if it remains in its place, then you will see Me." And when his Lord manifested Himself to the mountain, He made it as dust. And Moses fell down in a swoon. When he recovered his senses he said: "Glory be to You! to You I turn in repentance, and I am the first to believe."

He said: "I have chosen you above the people with My messages and My words, therefore take hold of what I have given to you and be of the grateful ones".

The Sovereignty 67:1-4

Exalted is He in Whose hands is the sovereignty ; who has power over all things ;

Who has created Death and Life, that He may try which of you is best in deed, and He is the Almighty, the Forgiving;"

He Who created the seven heavens one above another; No want of proportion will you see in the Creation of the Most Gracious. And turn your sight again; do you see any flaw?

Again turn your sight a second time; your sight will come back to you confused and exhausted.

The Cow 2:165

Yet there are men who take others besides God, as equal with Him; they love them as they should love God. But those of Faith are overflowing in their love for God. If only the unrighteous could see, behold, they would see the torment; that to God belongs all power, and God is severe in punishment.

Then those who were followed clear themselves of those who followed them ; They would see the torment, and all ties between them would be cut off.

The Unity 112

Say: He is God, the One and Only;
God, the Eternal, Absolute;
Never did He beget. Nor was He begotten.
And there is none like unto Him.

The Ornaments of Gold 43:84-85

It is He Who is God in heaven and God on earth; and He is full of Wisdom and Knowledge.

And blessed is He to Whom belongs the dominion of the heavens and the earth, and all between them: with Him is the Knowledge of the Hour (of Judgment): and to Him shall ye be brought back
.

The Kneeling 45:36-37

Then Praise be to God, Lord of the heavens and Lord of the earth,- Lord and Cherisher of all the Worlds!

To Him be glory throughout the heavens and the earth: and He is Exalted in Power, Full of Wisdom!

2. The Commandments

Cattle 6:151-155

151 Say: "Come, I will recite unto you what your Lord has made a sacred duty for you ": Do not associate anything with Him; be good to your parents; do kill not your children on a plea of want;- We provide sustenance for you and for them;- do not approach indecencies, whether open or secret; and do not kill a soul, which God has made sacred, except by way of justice and law.
That is what He has commanded you, that you may understand.

152 And come not nigh to the orphan's property, except to improve it, until he attain the age of full strength; give measure and weight with (full) justice;- no burden do We place on any soul, but that which it can bear; and whenever you speak, speak justly, even if a near relative is concerned; and fulfill the covenant of God; That is what He has commanded you, that you may remember.

153 Verily, this is My way, leading straight, follow it ; do follow not other paths; they will scatter you about from His path; That is what He has commanded you, that you may be righteous.

154 Moreover, We gave Moses the Book, completing Our favour to those who would do right, and explaining all things in detail,- and a guide and a mercy, that they might believe in the meeting with their Lord.
155 And this is a Book which We have revealed as a blessing; so follow it and be righteous, that you may receive mercy.

The Night Journey 17:23-39

23- Your Lord has decreed that you worship none but Him, and that you be kind to your parents. Whether one or both of them attain old age in your life, say not to them a word of contempt, nor repel them, but address them in terms of honor.

24- And, out of kindness, lower to them the wing of humility, and say: "My Lord! bestow on them thy Mercy as they cherished me in childhood."

25-Your Lord knows best what is in your hearts: If you do deeds of righteousness, verily He is Most Forgiving to those who turn to Him again and again in true penitence.

26- And render to the kindred their due rights -of alms, and to those in want, and to the wayfarer: But do not squander your wealth in the manner of a spendthrift.

27- Verily spendthrifts are brothers of the Evil Ones; and the devil was ever an ingrate to his Lord.

28 And even if you have to turn away from them in pursuit of the Mercy from your Lord which you do expect, yet speak to them a word of easy kindness.

29 And do not make your hand tied to you neck - like a niggard's, nor stretch it forth to its utmost reach, so that you become blameworthy and sorry.

30 Verily your Lord provides sustenance in abundance for whom He pleases, and He provides in a just measure. For He was ever Knower, Seer of all His servants.

31 And do not kill your children for fear of want: We shall provide sustenance for them as well as for you. Verily, killing them is a great sin.-

32 And do not come near unto adultery. For it is an abomination and an evil way.

33 And do not kill a soul - for God has made life sacred - except in the course of justice. And if anyone is slain wrongfully,- we have given his heir authority -to demand qisas or to forgive.
Thus, he shall not exceed the limits in avenging the murder; he will be helped.

34 Come not nigh to the orphan's property except to improve it, until he attains the age of full strength; and fulfill every engagement, for every engagement will be be questioned about.
35 Give full measure when you measure, and weigh with a balance that is straight;that is the most fitting and the most advantageous in the end.

36 And pursue not that of which you have no knowledge; for every act of hearing, or of seeing or of (feeling in) the heart will be enquired into (on the Day of Reckoning).

37 Nor walk on the earth with insolence ; for you can not rend the earth asunder, nor reach the mountains in height.

38 Of all such things the evil is hateful in the sight of your Lord.

39 These are among the precepts of wisdom, which your Lord has revealed to you. And do not take, with God, another object of worship, lest you should be thrown into Hell, blamed and rejected.

The Bee 16:90
The Bee 16:90 God commands justice, doing good, and generosity towards relatives, and He forbids immorality, and abomination and transgression. He advises you, so that you may take heed.

Luqman 31:12-19

12- We bestowed wisdom on Luqman: "Show your gratitude to God." Any who is (so) grateful does so to the profit of his own soul ; but if any is ungrateful, verily God is free of all wants, Worthy of all praise.

13-Behold, Luqman said to his son by way of instruction: "O my son! Do not associate partners in worship with God; for associating partners with God is a tremendous wrong."

14- And We have enjoined on man to honour his parents: his mother bears him in weakness upon weakness, and in years twain was his weaning: "Show gratitude to Me and to your parents ; to Me is your final Goal.

15- "But if they strive to make you join in worship with Me things of which you have no knowledge, do not obey them ; yet bear them company in this life with justice and consideration, and follow the way of those who turn to me in love ;in the end the return of you all is to Me, and I will tell you the truth and meaning of all that you did."

16-"O my son!" said Luqman, "If there be but the weight of a mustard-seed and it were hidden in a rock, or anywhere in the heavens or on earth, God will bring it forth ; for God is Subtile, All-Aware [understands the finest mysteries, and is well-acquainted with them]

17- "O my son! establish regular prayer, enjoin what is just, and forbid evil ; and bear with patient constancy whatever betide you ; that is of the steadfast heart of things

18- "And swell not your cheek at men [for pride], nor walk in insolence through the earth; for God does not love any arrogant boaster.

19-"And be moderate in your pace, and lower you voice; for the harshest of sounds without doubt is the braying of the ass."

3. The Faith

The Cow 2:1-5

A.L.M. This is the Book in which there is no doubt, a guidance for those who are mindful of God;

Who believe in the Unseen, are steadfast in prayer, and spend out of what We have provided for them;

And who believe in the Revelation sent to you, and sent before your time, and are certain of the Hereafter.

They are on true guidance from their Lord, and these will be the successful.

The Cow 2:177

Goodness is not that you turn your faces towards east or west;

but goodness is to believe in God and the Last Day, and the Angels, and the Book, and the Messengers;

to spend of your substance, out of love for Him, for your relatives, for orphans, for the needy, for the wayfarer, for those who ask, and for the ransom of slaves;

to be steadfast in prayer, and practice regular charity;

to fulfil the promise when you have made one ;

and to be firm and patient, in pain and adversity, and in times of danger.

Such are the people of truth, such are the God-fearing.

Women 4:57

57 But those who believe and do deeds of righteousness, We shall soon admit to Gardens, with rivers flowing beneath,- their eternal home ;Therein shall they have companions pure and holy, and We shall admit them to shades, cool and ever deepening.

Spoils of war 8:2-4

2- For, Believers are those who, when God is mentioned, feel a tremor in their hearts, and when they hear His signs rehearsed, find their faith strengthened, and put all their trust in their Lord;

3- Who establish regular prayers and spend freely out of the gifts We have given them for sustenance

4-Such in truth are the believers, they have grades of dignity with their Lord, and forgiveness, and generous sustenance.

The Believers 23:1-8

Successful are the believers

Those who humble themselves in their prayers;

And who avoid vain talk;

And who are active in deeds of charity;

And who guard their chastity,

Except for their spouses - that is, those whom they rightfully possess for (in their case) they are free from blame,

But those whose desires exceed those limits are transgressors;

And who Those who faithfully observe their trusts and engagements.

And who guard their prayers;

These will be the heirs,

Who will inherit Paradise wherein they abide forever.

The Ascending Stairways 70:19-35

19 Truly man was created very impatient;

20- Fretful when evil touches him;

21- And niggardly when good reaches him;

22- Except those who pray ;

23-Those who remain steadfast to their prayer;

24- And those in whose wealth is a recognised right (share)

25- For the needy who asks and the deprived ;

26- And those who believe in the Day of Judgement;

27- And those who fear the punishment of their Lord,

28- For their Lord's punishment is not to feel safe from

29- And those who guard their chastity,

30- Except with their wives whom their right hands possess,- for (then) they are not to be blamed,

31- But those who trespass beyond this are transgressors;

32- And those who respect their trusts and covenants;

33-And those who stand firm in their testimonies;

34- And those who observe their prayers ;

35- Such will be the honoured ones in the Gardens (of Bliss).

4. Prayer and Invocations from Quran

4.1.Prayer

The Opening 1:

1 In the name of God, Most Gracious, Most Merciful.

2 Praise be to God, Lord of the worlds;

3 Most Gracious, Most Merciful;

4 Master of the Day of Judgement.

5 You alone we worship; You alone we ask for help.

6 Show us the straight way,

7 The way of those on whom You Have bestowed Your Favours, not those against whom there is anger, nor of those who go astray.

The Cow 2:152

Then remember Me, I will remember you. Be thankful to Me, and do not be ungrateful to Me.

The Cow 2:238

Take care over doing your prayers, including the Middle Prayer; and stand before God in devotion.

Women 4:103

When you have performed the prayer, celebrate God's praises, standing, sitting down, or lying down on your sides; and when you are in safety, set up Regular Prayers; For such prayers are enjoined on believers at stated times.

Cattle 6:72

... To establish regular prayers and to fear God; for it is to Him that you will all be gathered together.

The Table 5:6

O you who believe! when you prepare for prayer, wash your faces, and your hands and arms to the elbows; Rub your heads with water; and wash your feet to the ankles. If you are in a state of ceremonial impurity, bathe your whole body. But if you are ill, or on a journey, or one of you comes from offices of nature, or you have been in contact with women, and you find no water, then take for yourselves clean sand or earth, and rub therewith your faces and hands, God does not wish to place you in a difficulty, but to make you clean, and to complete his favour to you, that you may be grateful.

The Spider 29:45

Recite what is revealed to you of the Book, and establish regular Prayer ; for Prayer restrains from shameful and unjust deeds; and remembrance of God is the greatest (thing in life) without doubt. And God knows what you do

4.2.Invocations of the Quran

The Cow 2:186, 201, 286

186- When My servants ask you concerning Me, I am indeed near

;I answer to the prayer of every suppliant when he calls on Me; Let them also respond to Me, and believe in Me so that they may be guided in the right way.

201- And there are some among them who say, "Our Lord, give us goodness in this world, and goodness in the Hereafter, and guard us from the torment of the Fire."

286- On no soul does God Place a burden greater than it can bear. It gets every good that it earns, and it suffers every ill that it earns. (Pray:) "Our Lord! Condemn us not if we forget or fall into error; our Lord! Lay not on us a burden Like that which You did lay on those before us; Our Lord! Lay not on us a burden greater than we have strength to bear. Blot out our sins, and grant us forgiveness. Have mercy on us. You are our Lord ; Help us against those who deny the truth."

The Family of Imran 2:8
"Our Lord! Let not our hearts deviate now after You have guided us, but grant us mercy from Your Presence; for You are the Grantor of bounties without measure.

The Cave 18:10
Behold, the youths betook themselves to the Cave;they said, "Our Lord! bestow on us Mercy from Yourself, and dispose of our affair for us in the right way!"

The Night Journey 17:110-111
Say: "Call upon God, or call upon The Most Gracious, by whatever name you call upon Him, it is well; for to Him belong the Most Beautiful Names. Neither speak your Prayer aloud, nor speak it too quiet but seek a middle course between.

And say, "Praise be to God, who begets no son, and has no

partner in sovereignty, nor needs He any to protect Him from weakness, and magnify Him for His greatness and glory "

Taha 20:25-28, 33-34

25 (Moses) said: "O my Lord! expand me my breast;

26 "Ease my task for me;

27 "And remove the impediment from my speech,

28 "So they may understand what I say;

29 "And give me a Minister from my family,

30 "Aaron, my brother;

31 "Add to my strength through him,

32 "And make him share my task;

33 "That we may celebrate Your praise without stint,

34 "And remember You without stint;

35 "For You are ever Seeing us."

4.3.Remembrance of God

The Cow 2:152

Then remember Me, I will remember you. Be thankful to Me, and do not ungrateful to Me.

Taha 20:42

"Go, thou and your brother, with My Signs, and slacken not, in keeping Me in remembrance.

The Clans 33:35, 41-43

35 For Muslims (men and women who have surrendered [to God]),- for believing men and women, for devout men and women, for true men and women, for men and women who are patient and constant, for men and women who humble themselves, for men and women who give in Charity, for men and women who fast, for men and women who guard their chastity,

and for men and women who engage much in God's remembrance and praise,- for them has God prepared forgiveness and great reward.

41 O you who believe! Celebrate the praises of God, and do this often;

42 And glorify Him morning and evening.

43 it is He Who sends blessings on you, as do His angels, that He may bring you out from the depths of Darkness into Light; and He is Full of Mercy to the Believers.

The Thunder 13:28

"Those who believe, and whose hearts find satisfaction in the remembrance of God; for without doubt in the remembrance of God do hearts find satisfaction [peace].

Light 24:41

Do you not see that God is He Whom do glorify all beings in the heavens and on earth, and the birds (of the air) with wings outspread? Each one knows its own mode of prayer and praise. And God knows well all that they do.

The Night Journey 17:44

The seven heavens and the earth, and all beings therein, declare His glory; there is not a thing but celebrates His praise; And yet you do not understand their praises! Verily He is Forbearing, Most Forgiving!

5. Charity

The Cow 2:254, 261-264, 245, 267-268, 271, 273-274

254- O you who believe! Spend out of what We have provided for you, before the Day comes when no bargaining, nor friendship nor intercession. Those who deny are the wrong-doers.

261- The parable of those who spend their substance in the way of God is that of a grain of corn; it grows seven ears, and each ear Has a hundred grains. God gives manifold increase to whom He pleases; And God is Bounteous and All-Knowing.

262- Those who spend their substance in the cause of God, and follow not up their gifts with reminders of their generosity or with injury,-for them their reward is with their Lord ; on them shall be no fear, nor shall they grieve.

263- Kind words and the covering of faults are better than charity followed by injury. God is free of all wants, and He is Most-Forbearing.

264-O you who believe! cancel not your charity by reminders of your generosity or by injury,- like those who spend their substance to be seen of men, but believe neither in God nor in the Last Day. They are in parable like a hard, barren rock, on which is a little soil; on it falls heavy rain, which leaves it just a bare stone. They will be able to do nothing with aught they have earned. And God does not guide those who deny the truth.

245- Who is he that will loan to God a beautiful loan, which God will double unto his credit and multiply many times? It is God that who provides and withholds, and to Him shall be your return.

267-O you who believe! Give of the good things which you have honourably earned, and of the fruits of the earth which We have produced for you, and do not even aim at getting anything which is bad, in order that out of it you may give away something, when you yourselves would not receive it except with closed eyes. And know that God is Free of all wants, and worthy of all praise.

268- The Evil one promises you with poverty and bids you to immorality. But God promises you His forgiveness and bounties. And God All-Embracing, All-knowing.

271- If you disclose acts of charity, even so it is well, but if you conceal them, and make them reach those really in need, that is better for you; And He will then remit from you many of your evil deeds. And God is well acquainted with what you do.

273- ... And whatever of good you give, be assured God knows it well.

274- Those who in charity spend of their goods by night and by day, in secret and in public, have their reward with their Lord; on them shall be no fear, nor shall they grieve.

The Heights 7:155-156

7:155 And Moses chose seventy of his people for Our place of meeting; when they were seized with violent quaking, he prayed: "O my Lord! if it had been Your will You could have destroyed, long before, both them and me; would You destroy us for the deeds of the fooliseeh ones among us? this is no more than Your trial; by it You cause whom You will to stray, and You lead whom You will into the right path. You are our Protector; so forgive us and give us Your mercy; for You are the best forgiver.

156- "And ordain for us that which is good, in this life and in the Hereafter; for we have turned unto You." He said: "As for My punishment, I smite with it whomever I will. But My mercy extends to all things, I shall therefore ordain it for those who do right, and practice regular charity, and those who believe in Our signs.

Repentance 9:60

Alms are for the poor and the needy, and those employed to administer the funds; for those whose hearts have been reconciled to Truth; for those in bondage and in debt; in the cause of God; and for the wayfarer; this is an ordinance from God, and God is full of knowledge and wisdom.

The Night Journey 17:26-29, 100

26- And render to the kindred their due rights -of alms, and to those in want, and to the wayfarer; But do not squander your wealth in the manner of a spendthrift.

27- Verily spendthrifts are brothers of the Evil Ones; and the devil was ever an ingrate to his Lord.

28 And even if you have to turn away from them in pursuit of the Mercy from your Lord which you do expect, yet speak to them a word of easy kindness.

29 And do not make your hand tied to you neck - like a niggard's, nor stretch it forth to its utmost reach, so that you become blameworthy and sorry.

The Night Journey 17:100

100- Say: "If you had control of the Treasures of the Mercy of my Lord, behold, you would keep them back, for fear of spending them; for man was ever niggardly "

The Criterion 25:67

Those who, when they spend, are not extravagant and not niggardly, but hold a just balance between those extremes.

Iron 57:7

Believe in God and His Messenger, and spend from what He has made you trustees heirs. For those of you who believe and spend will have a great reward.

The Hypocrites 63:10

And spend of that wherewith We have provided you before death comes unto one of you and he should say: My Lord! If only You would reprieve me for a little while, then I would give alms and be among the righteous.

The Romans 30:38-40

38- So give what is due [of charity] to relatives, the needy, and the wayfarer. That is better for those who seek the Countenance of God, and it is they who will be successful.

39- That which you give in usury for increase through the property of (other) people, will have no increase with God; but that which you lay out for charity, seeking the Countenance of God will increase; it is these who will get a recompense multiplied.

The Night 92:5-7

So he who gives in charity and fears God,
And in all sincerity testifies to the best,-
We will indeed smooth his way towards ease.
But he who is a greedy miser and thinks himself self-sufficient,
And gives the lie to the best,
We will indeed make smooth for him the path to Misery;
Nor will his wealth profit him when he falls headlong [into the Pit].

Gathering 64:15-17

15 Your possessions and your children may be but a trial. Whereas with God, is the highest reward.

16- So be mindful of God as much as you can; listen and obey and spend in charity for the benefit of your own soul and those saved from their own greed, such are the successful.

17- If you loan to God, a beautiful loan, He will double it to your credit, and He will grant you Forgiveness; for God is Most Appreciating, Most Forbearing,

The Dawn 89:15-26

15- Now, as for man, when his Lord tries him, giving him honour and gifts, then he says "My Lord hath honoured me."

16-But when He tries him, restricting his subsistence for him, then saith he (in despair), "My Lord has humiliated me!"

17- Nay, nay! but you do not honour the orphans!

18- Nor do you encourage one another to feed the poor!

137

19- And you devour inheritance - all with greed,

20- And you love wealth with inordinate love!

21-Nay! When the earth is pounded to powder,

22- And thy Lord comes, and His angels, rank upon rank,

23- And Hell, that Day, is brought (face to face),- on that Day will man remember, but how will that remembrance profit him?

24- He will say: "Ah! Would that I had sent forth good deeds for (this) my Future Life!"

The Heights 7:56
Do no mischief on the earth, after it has been set in order, but call on Him with fear and longing (in your hearts); for the Mercy of God is always near to those who do good.

The Cow 2:195
195- And spend of your substance in the cause of God, and make not your own hands contribute to your destruction; but do good; for God loves those who do good.

Abraham 14:31
Tell my servants who have believed, that they should establish regular prayers, and spend in charity out of the sustenance we have given them, secretly and openly, before the coming of a Day in which there will be neither mutual bargaining nor befriending.

The Family of Imran 3:133-134
Be quick in the race for forgiveness from your Lord, and for a Garden whose width is that of the whole of the heavens and of the earth, prepared **for the righteous,**

Those who spend freely, whether in prosperity, or in adversity; who restrain anger, and pardon people ; for God loves the doers of good;

And those who, when they commit a shameful deed, or wronged their own souls, earnestly bring God to mind, and ask for forgiveness for their sins,- and who can forgive sins except God?-

and are never obstinate in persisting knowingly in the wrong they have done.

For such the reward is forgiveness from their Lord, and Gardens with rivers flowing underneath,- an eternal dwelling; How excellent a recompense for those who work and strive!

Proscription of usury

The Cow 2:275- 276

275- Those who devour usury will not stand except as stand one whom the Evil one by his touch has driven to madness. That is because they say: "Trade is like usury," but God has permitted trade and forbidden usury. Those who after receiving direction from their Lord, desist, shall be pardoned for the past; their case is for God [to judge]; but those who repeat (The offense) are companions of the Fire; They will abide therein.

276- God will deprive usury of all blessing, but will give increase for deeds of charity; For He does not love creatures ungrateful and wicked.

6. Fasting

The Cow 2:183-185

183 O you who believe! Fasting is prescribed to you as it was prescribed to those before you, that you   that you become righteous

184 (Fasting) for a fixed number of days; but if any of you is ill, or on a journey, the prescribed number [should be made up] from days later. For those who can do it [With hardship], is a ransom, the feeding of one that is indigent. But he that will give more, of his own free will,-it is better for him.

And it is better for you that you fast, if you only knew.

185 Ramadan is the (month) in which the Quran was revealed, as a guide to mankind, also clear signs for guidance and judgment [Between right and wrong]. So every one of you who is present during that month should spend it in fasting, but if any one is ill, or on a journey, the prescribed period (Should be made up) by days later. God wishes for you convenience, not hardship, that you may complete the prescribed period, and to glorify Him in that He has guided you; and that you may be grateful.

7. The pilgrimage

The Cow 2:158, 195, 202

158- Behold! Safa and Marwa are among the Symbols of God. So if those who visit the House in the Season or at other times, should compass them round, it is no sin in them. And if any one obeys his own impulse to good,- be sure that God is All-Appreciating, All-knowing.

197 For Hajj are the months well known. If any one undertakes that duty therein, Let there be no obscenity, nor wickedness, nor wrangling in the Hajj. And whatever good you do, (be sure) God knows it. And take a provision [with you] for the journey, **but the best of provisions is right conduct**. So fear Me, O men of understanding.

198 There is no sin on you if you seek of the bounty of your Lord [during pilgrimage]. Then when you pour down from [Mount] Arafat, celebrate the praises of God at the Sacred Monument, and celebrate His praises as He has directed you, even though, before this, you went astray.

199 Then pass on at a quick pace from the place whence it is usual for the multitude so to do, and ask for God's forgiveness. For God is Oft-forgiving, Most Merciful.

200 So when ye have accomplished your holy rites, celebrate the praises of God, as you used to celebrate the praises of your fathers,- yea, with far more Heart and soul. There are men who say: "Our Lord! Give us Your bounties in this world!" but they will have no portion in the Hereafter.

201- And there are some among them who say, "Our Lord, give us goodness in this world, and goodness in the Hereafter, and guard us from the torment of the Fire."

202- To these will be allotted what they have earned; and God is quick in account.

The pilgrimage 22:26, 33-34
Behold! We gave the site, to Abraham, of the Sacred House, saying: Do not associate anything in worship with Me; and sanctify My House for those who compass it round, or stand up, or bow, or prostrate themselves.

And proclaim the Pilgrimage among men; they will come to you on foot and on every kind of camel, lean on account of journeys through deep and distant mountain highways;

That they may witness the benefits provided for them, and celebrate the name of God, through the Days appointed, over the cattle which He has provided for them ; then eat from it and feed the unfortunate poor.
Then let them complete the rites prescribed for them, perform their vows, and again circumbulate the Ancient House."

Such (is the Pilgrimage); whoever honours the sacred rites of

God, for him it is good in the Sight of his Lord. Lawful to you for food in Pilgrimage are cattle, except those mentioned to you ; but shun the abomination of idols, and shun the word that is false.

Being true in faith to God, and never assigning partners to Him; if anyone assigns partners to God, is as if he had fallen from heaven and been snatched up by birds, or the wind had swooped (like a bird on its prey) and thrown him into a far- distant place.

The Family Of 'Imran 3:96-97
The first House (of worship) appointed for men was that at Bakka; Full of blessing and of guidance for all kinds of beings.
In it are Signs Manifest; the Station of Abraham; whoever enters it attains security; Pilgrimage thereto is a duty men owe to God,- those who can afford the journey; but if any denies faith, God stands not in need of any of His creatures.

8. Learning and Knowledge in Islam

The Clot / Read! 96:1-5
Read, in the name of your Lord, who created
He created man, out of a clot
Read! And your Lord is Most Generous
He Who taught by means of the pen,-
He Taught man what he never knew.

The Family of Imran 2:18
There is no god but He; That is the witness of God, His angels, and those endowed with knowledge, standing firm on justice. There is no god but He, the Exalted in Power, the Wise.

She That Disputeth 58:11
... God will rise up, to suitable ranks [and degrees], those of you

who believe and who have been granted Knowledge. And God is well- acquainted with all you do.

Taha 20:114
... O my Lord! advance me in knowledge.

The Angels 35:27-28
See you not that God sends down rain from the sky? With it We then bring out produce of various colors. And in the mountains are tracts white and red, of various shades of colour, and black intense in hue.

And so among men and crawling creatures and cattle, are they of various colours. Among His servants, those who are endowed with knowledge, stand in true awe of God. For God is Exalted in Might, Oft-Forgiving.

The Spider 29:43
And such are the Parables We set forth for mankind, but none will understand their meaning save those who have knowledge.

9. Work

The Earthquake 99:1-8
1 When the earth is shaken to her (utmost) convulsion,

2-And the earth throws up her burdens (from within),

3-And man cries (distressed): 'What is the matter with her?'

4-On that Day will she declare her tidings.

5-For that your Lord will have inspired her.

6- On that Day will men proceed in companies sorted out, to be shown their deeds.

7-Then shall anyone who has done an atom's weight of good, see it!

8- And anyone who has done an atom's weight of evil, shall see it.

Repentance 9:105

And say: "Work ; Soon will God observe your work, and His Messenger, and the Believers"

Soon will you be brought back to the Knower of what is hidden and what is open; then will He show you the truth of all that you did."

Women 4:124

If any do deeds of righteousness,- be they male or female – while believing, such will enter paradise and they will not be wronged the dint in a date-stone.

The Family Of Imran 3:30

The Family of Imran 3:30 "On the Day when every soul will find all the good it has done, and as for the evil it has done, it will wish there were far, far away. And God cautions you (To remember) Himself. And God is compassionate towards His servants.

The Thunder 13:29

For those who believe and work righteousness, is every blessedness, and a beautiful place of return.

The Bee 16:97

Whoever works righteousness, man or woman, and has Faith, verily, We shall grant him a good life, and reward them according to the best of their actions.

The Congregation 62:10

And when the Prayer is finished, then may you spread through the land, and seek of the Bounty of God, and celebrate the Praises of God often that you may prosper.

Luqman 31:16

"O my son!" (said Luqman), "If there be (but) the weight of a mustard-seed and it were (hidden) in a rock, or (anywhere) in the heavens or on earth, God will bring it forth; for God understands the finest mysteries, (and) is well-acquainted (with them).

The Prostration 32:17

Now no person knows what delights of the eye are kept hidden in reserve for them - as a reward for their good deeds.

10. Honesty in Work

Defrauding (The Cheats) 83:1-3

Woe to those that deal in fraud,-

Those who, when they have to receive by measure from men, demand full measure,

But when they have to give by measure or weight to men, give less than due

Do they not think that they will be called to account?

On a Mighty Day,

Hud 11:84-86

84- To the Madyan People (We sent) Shu'aib, one of their own brethren; he said: "O my people! worship God ; You have no other god but Him. And give not short measure or weight; I see you in prosperity, but I fear for you the penalty of a day that will compass (you) all round.

85- "And O my people! give just measure and weight, nor withhold from the people the things that are their due; commit not evil in the land with intent to do mischief.

86- "That which is left you by God [no matter how small] is better for you, if you believed! and I am not a keeper over you. "

The Poets 26 :175-191

176 The Companions of the Wood rejected the apostles.

177 Behold, Shu'aib said to them: "Will you not fear God?

178 "I am to you a messenger worthy of all trust.

179 "So fear God and obey me.

180 "No reward do I ask of you for it; my reward is only from the Lord of the Worlds.

181 "Give just measure, and cause no loss [to others by fraud].

182 "And weigh with scales true and upright.

183 "And withhold not things justly due to men, nor do evil in the land, working mischief.

184 "And fear Him Who created you and [who created] the generations before you"

185 They said: "You are only one of those bewitched!

186 "You are no more than a mortal like us, and indeed we think you are a liar!

187 "Now cause a piece of the sky to fall on us, if you are truthful!"

188 He said: "My Lord knows better what you do."

189 But they rejected him. Then the punishment of a day of overshadowing gloom seized them, and that was the Penalty of a Great Day.

190 Verily in that is a Sign; but most of them do not believe.

191 And verily your Lord is He, the Exalted in Might, Most Merciful.

The Table 5:1 O you who believe! fulfil your obligations.

The Most Gracious (The Beneficent) 55:1-9

1 (God) Most Gracious!

2 It is He Who has taught the Qur'an.

3 He has created man:

4 He has taught him speech [and intelligence].

5 The sun and the moon follow their calculated courses ;

6 And the herbs and the trees - both alike bow in adoration.

7 And the Firmament has He raised high, and He has set up the Balance,

8 In order that you may not transgress (due) balance.

9 So establish weight with justice and fall not short in the balance.

11. Moral values

Good words

Women 4:148 God does not like bad words to be made in public, except when one is treated with injustice ; For God is All-Hearing, All-Seeing

Abraham 14:24-27

24-Do you not see how God sets forth a parable? - - A goodly word like a goodly tree, whose root is firmly fixed, and its branches are high in the sky. It brings forth its fruit at all times, by the leave of its Lord. And God sets forth parables for people so that they may reflect.

26 And the parable of an evil Word is that of an evil tree; It is torn up by the root from the surface of the earth; it has no stability.

27 God will establish in strength those who believe, with the word that stands firm, in this world and in the Hereafter; but God will leave, to stray, those who do wrong and God does what He wills.

The Clans 33:70-71

70 O you who believe! Fear God, and say words straight to the point;

71 That He may make your conduct whole and sound and forgive you your sins. And whoever obeys God and His Apostle, has already attained the highest achievement.

The Cow 2:83

And remember We took a covenant from the Children of Israel : Worship none but God; treat with kindness your parents and kindred, and orphans and those in need; **speak fair to the people**; be steadfast in prayer; and practice regular charity.

The Night Journey 17:53

Say to My servants that they should only say those things that are the best, for Satan does sow dissensions among them; For Satan is to man an avowed enemy.

Women 4:86

When a [courteous] greeting is offered you, meet it with a greeting still more courteous, or at least of equal courtesy. God takes careful account of all things.

Luqman 31:19

"And be moderate in your pace [walk humbly], and lower your voice "

The Private Apartments 49:2-3

2 O you who believe! Raise not your voices above the voice of the Prophet, nor speak aloud to him in talk, as you may speak aloud to one another, lest your deeds become vain and you perceive not.

3 Those that lower their voices in the presence of God's Messenger,- are the ones whose hearts God has God tested for piety ; for them is Forgiveness and a great Reward.

Equity and Justice

Iron 57:25

We sent aforetime our messengers with clear signs [proofs] and sent down with them the Book and the Balance (of Right and Wrong), that men may stand forth in justice

Cattle 6:152
152 And whenever you speak, speak justly, even if a near relative is concerned;

The Bee 16:90
God commands justice, doing good, and generosity towards relatives, and He forbids immorality, and abomination and transgression. He advises you, so that you may take heed.

Women 4:135
O you who believe! stand out firmly for justice, as witnesses to God, even towards yourselves, or your parents, or your relatives, and whether it be (against) rich or poor; for God can best protect both. Follow not the your low desires, lest you deviate from justice, and if you distort your witness or disregard [this commandment], verily God is well-acquainted with all that you do.

The Table 5:8
O you who believe! stand out firmly for God, as witnesses to fair dealing, and let not the hatred of others to you make you swerve to wrong and depart from justice. Be just; that is next to piety; and fear God. For God is well-acquainted with all that you do.

Up-rightness

Hud 11:112
Therefore stand firm in the straight Path as you have been commanded, together with those who turn with you in repentance [unto God]; and transgress not [from the Path] ; for He is All-Seer

of what you do.

(Signs) Spelled Out 41:30-33

30 In the case of those who say, "Our Lord is God", and, further, **stand straight and steadfast**, the angels descend on them : "Have no fear or grief! but receive the Glad Tidings of the Paradise you were promised!

31 "We are your protectors in this life and in the Hereafter; therein shall you have all that your souls shall desire; and therein shall you have all that you ask for.

32 "A hospitable gift from one Oft-Forgiving, Most Merciful!"

33 Who speaks better than one who calls to God, works righteousness, and says, "I am one of the submitters"?

Mutual Consultation 42:15

So [Prophet], call to the Faith, and stand in the straight path as you have been commanded, and do not follow their vain desires; but say: "I believe in the Book which God has sent down; and I am commanded to judge justly between you. God is our Lord and your Lord. We have our deeds, and you have your deeds. There is no contention between us and you. God will bring us together, and to Him is our Final Goal.

The Wind-Curved Sandhills 46:12-14

12 And before this, was the Book of Moses as a guide and a mercy. And this is Book confirming it in the Arabic language to admonish the unjust, and as Glad Tidings to the good-doers.

13 Verily those who say, "Our Lord is God," **and remain firm in the straight path**, there is no fear, nor shall they grieve.

14 They will be the Companions of the Paradise, dwelling therein, a recompense for their good deeds.

Proscription of gossips, spying on each other behind their backs

The private Apartments 49:12 ... O you who believe! Avoid suspicion as much as possible ; for suspicion in some cases is a sin. And do not spy on each other behind their backs nor shall you backbite one another.

Women 4:114 There is no good , in most of their secret talks, except if one exhorts to a deed of charity or justice or conciliation between men; To anyone who does this, seeking the good pleasure of God, We shall soon give a reward of the highest value.

She That Disputeth 58:7, 9-10

7 Do you not see that God does know all that is in the heavens and on earth? There is not a secret consultation between three, but He makes the fourth among them, - Nor between five but He makes the sixth,- nor between fewer nor more, but He is in their midst, wheresoever they be; In the end will He tell them the truth of their conduct, on the Day of Judgement. For God is All-Knower of everything.

9 O you who believe! When you hold secret counsel, do not do it for iniquity and hostility, and disobedience to the Prophet; but do it for righteousness and self-restraint; and fear God, to Whom you shall be brought back.

10 Secret counsels are only inspired by the Evil One, in order that he may cause grief to the Believers; but he cannot harm them in the least, except as God permits; and on God let the Believers put their trust.

151

Observing Trusts

Women 4:58 God commands you to render back the trusts to those to whom they are due; And when you judge between people, that you judge with justice; Verily how excellent is the teaching which He gives you! For God is All-Hearing, All-Seeing

The Believers 23:1-8 Successful are the believers ... Those who faithfully observe their trusts and engagements.

Showing Gratitude for the Favours of God

The Cow 2:152
Then remember Me, I will remember you. Be thankful to Me, and do not be ungrateful to Me.

172 O you who believe! Eat of the good things that We have provided for you, and be grateful to God, if you do worship Him.

Abraham 14:7
And remember! your Lord proclaimed: "If you are grateful, I will add more favours unto you; But if you show ingratitude, then My punishment is severe indeed."

The Bees 16:120-123
Abraham was indeed a model, devoutly obedient to God, and true in Faith, and was not of those who ascribe divinity to aught beside God.
He showed his gratitude for the favours of God, Who chose him, and guided him to a Straight Way.
And We gave him his reward in this world, and he will be, in the Hereafter, in the ranks of the Righteous.
So We have revealed to you: "Follow the ways of Abraham who was the True in Faith, and was not of those who ascribe divinity

to aught beside God."

Cattle 6:53

Thus did We try some of them by comparison with others, that they should say: "Are these the people that God has favoured from among us?" Is God not the most aware of the grateful ones ?

The Heights 7:10

10 It is We Who have placed you with authority on earth, and provided you therein with means for the fulfillment of your life. But little give you thanks.

The Bees 16:78

It is He Who brought you forth from the wombs of your mothers when you knew nothing; and He gave you hearing and sight and intelligence and affections; that you may give thanks (to God)...

The Ant 27:73

But verily your Lord is full of grace to mankind. Yet most of them are ungrateful.

Yasin 36:71-73

71 See they not that it is We Who have created for them - among the things which Our hands have fashioned - cattle, which are under their dominion?-

72 And that We have subjected them to their use? of them some do carry them and some they eat.

73 And they have other profits from them besides, and they get milk to drink. Will they not then be grateful?

Patience and Perseverance

The Family Of Imran 3:200
O you who believe! Persevere in patience and constancy; vie in such perseverance; strengthen each other; and fear God; that you may be successful.

Muhammad 47:31
And We shall try you until We test those among you who strive their utmost and persevere in patience; and We shall try your reported mettle.

The Cow 2:153, 155-157
O you who believe! seek help with patient perseverance and prayer; for God is with those who patiently persevere.
155 Be sure we shall test you with something of fear and hunger, some loss in goods or lives or the fruits (of your toil), but give glad tidings to those who patiently persevere,
156 Who say, when afflicted with calamity: "To God We belong, and to Him is our return":
157 They are those on whom (Descend) blessings from God, and Mercy, and they are the ones that receive guidance.

The Cow 2:177 ...
and to be firm and patient, in pain and adversity, and in times of danger. Such are the people of truth, the God-fearing.

Moderation

The Cow 2:143
Thus, have We made of you a moderate community justly balanced that you might be witnesses over the nations, and the messenger a witness over yourselves.

The Night Journey 17:29
And do not make your hand tied to you neck - like a niggard's, nor stretch it forth to its utmost reach, so that you become blameworthy and sorry.

The Criterion 25:67
Those who, when they spend, are not extravagant and not niggardly, but hold a just balance between those extremes.

Cattle 6:141
141 It is He Who has produced gardens, with trellises and without, and dates, and tilth with produce of all kinds, and olives and pomegranates, similar in kind and different in variety : eat of their fruit in their season, but render the dues that are proper on the day that the harvest is gathered. But waste not by excess; for God does not love the wasters.

Fulfilment of Commitments and Contracts

The Table 5:1
O you who believe! fulfil your obligations.

The Cow 2:177 Goodness is not that you turn your faces towards east or west;
but goodness is to believe in God and the Last Day, and the Angels, and the Book, and the Messengers;
to spend of your substance, out of love for Him, for your relatives, for orphans, for the needy, for the wayfarer, for those who ask, and for the ransom of slaves;
to be steadfast in prayer, and practice regular charity;
to fulfil the promise when you have made one ;
and to be firm and patient, in pain and adversity, and in times of danger.
Such are the people of truth, the God-fearing.

The Bee 16:91

Fulfill the Covenant of God when you have made it, and break not your oaths after you have confirmed them; indeed you have made God your surety; for God knows all that you do.

The Family Of Imran 3:75-76

75 Among the People of the Book are some who, if entrusted with a hoard of gold, will readily pay it back; others, who, if entrusted with a single silver coin, will not repay it unless you constantly stood demanding, because, they say, "We have no duty to the Gentiles. But they tell a lie concerning God knowingly.
76 Nay.- Those who fulfill their pledges and act aright,-verily God loves the righteous.

Enjoining what is right, and forbidding what is wrong

The Family of Imran 3:104, 110

Let there arise out of you a community inviting to all that is good, enjoining what is right, and forbidding the evil. These are the successful.

Modesty

The Story 28:76-78 , 83

76 Qarun was doubtless, of the people of Moses; but he acted insolently towards them; such were the treasures We had bestowed on him that their very keys would have been a burden to a body of strong men, behold, his people said to him: "Exult not , for God does not love the exultant (in riches).
77 "But seek, with the (wealth) which God has bestowed on thee, the Home of the Hereafter, nor forget your portion in this world

and do good to others, as God has been good to you, and seek not occasions for mischief in the land; for God does not love those who do mischief."

78 He said: "This has been given to me because of a certain knowledge which I have." Did he not know that God had destroyed, before him, (whole) generations,- which were superior to him in strength and greater in the amount of riches they had collected? but the wicked are not called [immediately] to account for their sins.

83 That Home of the Hereafter We shall give to those who intend not high- handedness or mischief on earth; and the end is best for the righteous.

The Night Journey 17:37-38

37 Nor walk on the earth with insolence; for you can not rend the earth asunder, nor reach the mountains in height.
38 Of all such things the evil is hateful in the sight of your Lord.

Repentance 9:25

Assuredly God did help you in many battle-fields and on the day of Hunain; Behold! your great numbers made you to proud, but they availed you naught; the land, for all that it is wide, did constrain you, and you turned back in retreat.

Proscription of Mockery

The private Apartments 49:11

O you who believe! Let not some men among you laugh at others, it may be that the latter are better than the former ; Nor let some women laugh at others, it may be that the latter are better than the former ; Nor defame nor be sarcastic to each other, nor call each other by offensive nicknames; Ill-seeming is a name connoting wickedness, to be used of one after he has believed. And those who do not desist are indeed doing wrong.

12. Tolerance in Islam

Tolerance between individuals

(Signs) Spelled Out 41:34-35

34 Nor can goodness and Evil be equal. Repel the evil deed with the best possible response. Then the one between whom and you there was enmity will your best friend and intimate!

35 And no one will be granted such goodness except those who exercise patience and self-restraint,- none but persons who are extremely fortunate.

The Family Of Imran 3:133-134

Be quick in the race for forgiveness from your Lord, and for a Garden whose width is that of the whole of the heavens and of the earth, prepared **for the righteous,**

Those who spend freely, whether in prosperity, or in adversity; **who restrain anger, and pardon people** ; for God loves the doers of good;

Mutual Consultation 42:40-43

40 The recompense for an injury is an injury equal thereto (in degree); but if a person forgives and makes reconciliation, his reward is due from God; for (God) does not love the wrong-doers.

41 But indeed if any do help and defend themselves after a wrong done to them, against such there is no cause of blame.

42 The blame is only against those who oppress men and wrong-doing and insolently transgress beyond bounds through the land, defying right and justice; for such there will be a penalty grievous.

43 But indeed if any show patience and forgive, that would truly be an exercise of courageous will and resolution in the conduct of

affairs.

Light 24:22
... Let them forgive and overlook, do you not wish that God should forgive you? For God is Oft-Forgiving, Most Merciful.

The Family Of Imran 3:159
It is part of the Mercy of God that you do deal gently with them had you been severe or harsh-hearted, they would have broken away from about you ; so pass over (their faults), and ask forgiveness for them; and consult them in affairs. Then, when you have taken a decision put your trust in God. For God loves the trusting.

Tolerance at collective level

The Private Apartments 49:13
O mankind! We created you from a male and a female, and made you into nations and tribes, that you may know each other. Verily the most honoured of you in the sight of God is **the most righteous of you**. And God is All-Knowing, All-Aware

Women 4:1
O mankind! reverence your Lord, who created you from a single person, and created from it, His mate, and from them twain scattered countless men and women;- reverence God, through whom you demand your mutual rights, and reverence the wombs [That bore you]; for God has ever been a watcher over you.

Diversity in the World

The Romans 30:22
And among His Signs is the creation of the heavens and the earth, and the variations in your languages and your colours; verily in that are Signs for those who know.

The Table 5:44-48

44 We did reveal the Torah wherein was guidance and light. By its standard have been judged the Jews, by the prophets who submitted themselves to God's will, by the rabbis and the doctors of law; for to them was entrusted the protection of God's book, and they were witnesses thereto; therefore fear not men, but fear Me, and sell not My signs for a miserable price. If any do fail to judge by the light of what God has revealed ; such are the deniers [of truth].

45 We ordained therein for them: "Life for life, eye for eye, nose for nose, ear for ear, tooth for tooth, and wounds equal for equal." But if any one remits the retaliation by way of charity, it is an act of atonement for himself. And if any fail to judge by the light of what God hath revealed, such are the wrong-doers.

46 And in their footsteps We sent Jesus the son of Mary, confirming the Torah that had come before him, and We sent him the Gospel, therein was guidance and light, and confirming which was revealed in the Torah, and a guidance and an admonition to those who fear God.

47 Let the people of the Gospel judge by what God has been revealed therein. And whoever did not judge according to what God has revealed, such are the transgressors.

48 And We sent to you the Scripture in truth, confirming the scripture that came before it, and superseding it ; so judge between them by what God has revealed, and do not follow their vain desires, diverging from the Truth that has come to you. To each among you have We prescribed a law and an open way. *If God had so willed, He would have made you a single community, but He wishes to test you in what He has given you; so compete in virtuous deeds. The goal of you all is to God; it is He that will show you the truth of the matters in which you dispute;"*

Hud 11:118

If your Lord had so willed, He would have made all people a single community, but they will continue to have their differences.

Recognition by Islam of Previous Monotheist Religions

The Cow 2:1-4 , 62, 285

A.L.M. This is the Book in which there is no doubt, a guidance for those who fear God;

Who believe in the Unseen, are steadfast in prayer, and spend out of what We have provided for them;

And who believe in the Revelation sent to you, and sent before your time, and are certain of the Hereafter.

They are on true guidance from their Lord, and these will be the successful.

62 Those who believe in the Qur'an, those who follow the Jewish scriptures, and the the Christians, and the Sabians - any who believe in God and the Last Day, and work righteousness,- on them shall be no fear, nor shall they grieve.

285 The messenger believes in what has been revealed to him from his Lord, as do the men of faith. They all believe in God, His angels, His books, and His messengers. "We make no distinction (they say) between one and another of His messengers." And they say: "We hear, and we obey ; We seek Your forgiveness, our Lord, and to You is the end of all journeys."

The Pilgrimage 22:17

Those who believe in the Qur'an, those who follow the Jewish scriptures, and the Sabians, Christians, Magians, and Polytheists,- God will judge between them on the Day of Judgement; for God is witness of all things

The Appeal to Dialogue

The Spider 29:46
And do not argue with the people of the scripture (Jews, Christians, and Muslims) except in the best way, unless it be with those who act unjustly ; but say, "We believe in what was revealed to us and in that what was revealed to you; Our God and your God is one; and to Him we are submitters."

The family of Imran 3:64
Say: "O People of the Book! come to common terms as between us and you: That we worship none but God; that we associate no partners with Him; that we do not take, from among ourselves, Lords and patrons other than God." If then they turn back, then say : "Bear witness that we at least are submitted to God's Will.

No Compulsion in Religion

The Cow 2:256
Let there be no compulsion in religion; Truth stands out clear from Error; whoever rejects evil and believes in God has grasped the most trustworthy hand-hold, that never breaks. And God is All-Hearing All-Knowing.

The Cave 18:29
Say, "The truth is from your Lord": Then whoever wills, let him believe, and whoever wills let him reject it.

Jonah 10:99
If it had been your Lord's will, all the people on earth would have believed,- will you then compel mankind to believe!

Banning aggressions and transgressions

The Cow 2:190
Fight in the cause of God those who fight you, but do not commit aggression ; for God does not love the transgressors.

She That Is To Be Examined 60:8
God does not forbid you to deal kindly and justly with those who do not fight you for (your) Faith nor drive you out of your homes ; for God loves those who are just.

The Table 5:2, 32
2 ... and let not the hatred of some people who once prevented you from going to the Sacred Mosque lead you to transgression [or aggression]. And help one another in righteousness and piety, but do not help one another in sin and aggression and fear God ; for God is strict in punishment.

32 ... On that account, We ordained for the Children of Israel that if any one killed a person - unless it be for murder or for spreading mischief in the land - it would be as if he had killed the whole of mankind; and if any one saved a life, it would be as if he saved the life of the whole of mankind

13. Mistakes, Sins and repentance

Women 4:110-112, 149
110 If any one does evil or wrongs his own soul but afterwards seeks God's forgiveness, he will find God Oft-forgiving, Most Merciful.

111 And if any one earns sin, he earns it against his own soul; for God is All-Knowing, Most Wise.

112 But if any one earns a fault or a sin and then accuses of it one innocent, he carries on himself a falsehood and a flagrant sin.

149 Whether you publish a good deed or conceal it or pardon an evil, verily God is ever Pardoning, All-Powerful.

Cattle 6:54

And when those who believe in Our signs come to you, Say: "Peace be on you; Your Lord has inscribed for Himself the rule of mercy; verily, if any of you did evil in ignorance, and thereafter repented, and amend his conduct, lo! He is Oft- forgiving, Most Merciful.

The Heights 7:153

But those who do wrong but repent thereafter and (truly) believe,- verily your Lord is thereafter Oft-Forgiving, Most Merciful.

Hud 11:3, 52, 61

3 And Seek the forgiveness of your Lord, and turn to Him in repentance; that He may grant you a good enjoyment, for a term appointed, and bestow His abounding grace on every bountiful one. But if you turn away, then I fear for you the retribution of an awful Day

52 "And O my people! Ask forgiveness of your Lord, and turn to Him in repentance; He will send you the skies pouring abundant rain, and add strength to your strength; so do not turn back in sin!"

61 To the Thamud People (We sent) Salih, one of their own brethren. He said: "O my people! Worship God; you have no other god but Him. It is He Who has initiated you from the earth and settled you therein; then ask forgiveness of Him, and turn to Him in repentance; for my Lord is always near, ready to answer."

Taha 20:80-82

80 O Children of Israel! We delivered you from your enemy, and We made a Covenant with you on the right side of Mount (Sinai), and We sent down to you Manna and quails.

81 (Saying): "Eat of the good things We have provided for your sustenance, but commit no excess therein, lest My Wrath should justly descend on you ; and those on whom descends My Wrath do perish indeed!

82 "But, without doubt, I am Most forgiving to those who repent, believe, and do right, and in fine, remains guided."

The Clans 33:5

... But there is no blame on you if you make unintentionally a mistake therein ; what counts is the intention of your hearts, and God is Oft-Returning, Most Merciful.

Noah 71:1-7

1 We sent Noah to his People (with the Command): "warn thy People before there comes to them a painful retribution."

2 He said: "O my People! I am to you a Warner, clear and open;

3 "That you should worship God, fear Him and obey me;

4 "So He may forgive you your sins and give you respite for a stated term, for when the term given by God is accomplished, it cannot be put forward, if you only knew."

5 He said: "O my Lord! I have called to my People night and day.

6 "But my call only increases their flight from the Right.

7 "And every time I have called to them, that You might forgive them, they have only thrust their fingers into their ears, covered themselves up with their garments, grown obstinate, and given themselves up to arrogance"

8 "So I have called to them aloud;

9 "Further I have spoken to them in public and secretly in private,

10 "Saying, 'Ask forgiveness from your Lord; for He is Oft-Forgiving;

11 "'He will send rain to you in abundance;

12 "'Give you increase in wealth and sons; and bestow on you gardens and bestow on you rivers (of flowing water).

13 "'What is the matter with you, that you place not your hope for kindness and long-suffering in God,-

14 "'Seeing that it is He that has created you in diverse stages?

15 "'See you not how God has created the seven heavens one above another,

16 "'And made the moon a light in their midst, and made the sun as a (Glorious) Lamp?

17 "'And God has created you from the earth growing (gradually),

18 "'And in the End He will return you into the (earth), and raise you forth (again at the Resurrection)?

19 "'And God has made the earth for you as a carpet (spread out),

20 "'That you may go about therein, in spacious roads.'"

Banning 66:8

O you who believe! Turn to God with sincere repentance ; In the hope that your Lord will remit your sins and admit you to Gardens beneath which Rivers flow,- the Day that God will not disappoint the Prophet and those who believe with him. Their Light will run forward before them and by their right hands, while they say, "Our Lord! Perfect our Light for us, and grant us Forgiveness, for You are All-Powerful."

The Troops 39:53-54

53 Say: "O My Servants who have transgressed against their souls! Despair not of the Mercy of God, for God forgives all sins; for He is Oft-Forgiving, Most Merciful.

54 And Turn unto your Lord in repentance and surrender unto Him, before there come unto you the doom ; and you can not be helped.

14. The privilege of Man and his responsibility

The Night Journey 17:70-72

70 We have honoured the sons of Adam; provided them with transport on land and sea; given them for sustenance things good and pure; and conferred on them special favours, above a great part of our creation.

71 On the day when We shall call together all human beings with their leader ; those who are given their record in their right hand will read it, and they will not be dealt with unjustly in the least.

72 But those who were blind in this world, will be blind in the hereafter, and most astray from the Path.

Yasin 36:71-73

71 See they not that it is We Who have created for them - among the things which Our hands have fashioned - cattle, which are under their dominion?-

72 And that We have subjected them to their use? of them some do carry them and some they eat.

73 And they have other profits from them besides, and they get milk to drink. Will they not then be grateful?

Luqman 31:20

Do you not see that God has subjected to your use all things in the heavens and on earth, and has made his bounties flow to you in exceeding measure, both seen and unseen? Yet there are among men those who dispute about God, without knowledge or guidance or an illuminating book.

Abraham 14:7,34

7 And remember! your Lord proclaimed: "If you are grateful, I will add more favours unto you; But if you show ingratitude, then My punishment is severe indeed."

34 And He gives you of all that you ask for. But if you count the favours of God, never will you be able to number them. Verily, man is given up to injustice and ingratitude.

The Bee 16:3-18

3 He has created the heavens and the earth for just ends ; far is He above having the partners they ascribe to Him.

4 He has created man from a tiny drop; and behold this same man becomes an open disputer!

5 And cattle He has created for you (men); from them you derive warmth, and numerous benefits, and of their [meat] you eat.

6 And you have a sense of beauty in them as you drive them home in the evening, and as you lead them forth to pasture in the morning.

7 And they carry your heavy loads to lands that you could not reach except with souls distressed ; for your Lord is indeed Most Kind, Most Merciful,

8 And He has created horses, mules, and donkeys, for you to ride and use for show; and He has created other things of which you have no knowledge.

9 And unto God leads straight the Way, but there are ways that turn aside; if God had willed, He would have guided all of you.

10 It is He who sends down rain from the sky; from it you drink, and out of it grows the vegetation on which you feed your cattle.

11 With it He produces for you corn, olives, date-palms, grapes and every kind of fruit; verily in this is a sign for people who reflect.

12 He has made subject to you the Night and the Day; the sun and the moon; and the stars are in subjection by His Command; verily in this are Signs for men who are wise.

13 And the things on this earth which He has multiplied in varying colors and qualities ; verily in this is a sign for men who celebrate the praises of God in gratitude.

14 It is He Who has made the sea subject, that you may eat thereof flesh that is fresh and tender, and that you may extract therefrom ornaments to wear; and you see the ships therein that plough the waves, that you may seek thus of the bounty of God and that you may be grateful.

15 And He has set up on the earth mountains standing firm, lest it should shake with you; and rivers and roads; that you may guide yourselves;

16 And marks and sign-posts; and by the stars men guide themselves.

17 Is then One who creates like one who does not create? Would you now take heed?

18 If you would count up the favours of God, never would you be able to number them, for God is Oft-Forgiving, Most Merciful.

The Bee 16:53
Whatever blessing you enjoy is from God. And when you are touched by distress, unto Him you cry with groans;

15. The creation

The Cow 2:29-39
29 It is He Who has created for you all things that are on earth; Moreover His design comprehended the heavens, for He gave order and perfection to the seven firmaments; and of all things He has perfect knowledge.

30 Behold, your Lord said to the angels: "I will create a vicegerent on earth." They said: "Will You place therein one who will make mischief therein and shed blood?- while we do

celebrate Your praises and glorify Your holy name?" He said: "I know what you do not know."

31 And He taught Adam the names of all things; then He placed them before the angels, and said: "Tell me the names of these if you are right."

32 They said: "Glory to You, of knowledge we have none, save what You have taught us; In truth it is You Who are perfect in knowledge and wisdom."

33 He said: "O Adam! Tell them their names." When he had told them, God said: "Did I not tell you that I know the secrets of heaven and earth, and I know what you reveal and what you conceal?"

34 And behold, We said to the angels: "Bow down to Adam" and they bowed down. Not so Iblis; he refused and was too arrogant and he was of the disbelievers.

35 We said: "O Adam! dwell you and your wife in the Paradise ; and eat of the bountiful things therein as you will; but approach not this tree, lest you become wrong-doers."

36 Then did Satan make them slip from the (garden), and get them out of the state [of felicity] in which they had been. We said: "Fall down all of you, you [Man and Satan] are each other's enemy. On earth will be your dwelling-place and your means of livelihood - for a time."

37 Then Adam received from his Lord words of inspiration, and his Lord turned towards him; for He is Oft-Returning, Most Merciful.

38 We said: "Get down all from here; but if, as is sure, there comes to you Guidance from Me, whoever follows My guidance, on them shall be no fear, nor shall they grieve.

The Heights 7:11-28

11 And We created you and gave you shape; then We bade the angels bow down to Adam, and they bowed down; not so Iblis; He refused to be of those who bow down.

12 (God) said: "What prevented you from bowing down when I commanded you?" He said: "I am better than him; You create me from fire, and him from clay."

13 (God) said: "Get down from it ; it is not for you to be arrogant here; get out, for you are of the meanest (of creatures)."

14 He said: "Give me respite till the day they are raised up."

15 (God) said: "You are among those who have respite."

16 He said: "Because You have thrown me out of the way, lo! I will lie in wait for them on Your straight way.

17 "Then will I assault them from before them and behind them, from their right and their left, and You will not find most of them grateful [for Your mercies]."

18 (God) said: "Get out from this, disgraced and expelled. If any of them follow you,- Hell will I fill with you all.

19 "O Adam! dwell you and your wife in the Garden, and enjoy its good things as you wish; but do not approach this tree, or you run into harm and transgression."

20 Then Satan began to whisper suggestions to them, bringing openly before their minds all their shame that was hidden from them [before]; he said: "Your Lord only forbade you this tree, lest you should become angels or become of the immortals."

21 And he swore to them both, that he was their sincere adviser.

22 So he duped them by deceit ; and when they tasted of the tree, their shame became manifest to them, and they began to sew together the leaves of the garden over their bodies. And their Lord called unto them: "Did I not forbid you that tree, and tell you that Satan was an avowed enemy unto you?"

23 They said: "Our Lord! We have wronged our own souls, and if You do not forgive us not and bestow not upon us Your Mercy, we shall certainly be lost."

24 (God) said: "Get down with enmity between yourselves [Man

and Satan]. On earth will be your dwelling-place and your means of livelihood,- for a time."

25 He said: "Therein you will live, and therein you will die; and from you will be taken out."

26 O Children of Adam! We have bestowed raiment upon you to cover your shame, as well as to be an adornment to you. But the raiment of righteousness is the best. Such are among the Signs of God, that they may receive admonition!

27 O Children of Adam! Let not Satan seduce you, in the same manner as He got your parents out of the Paradise, stripping them of their raiment, to expose their shame; for he and his tribe watch you from a position where you cannot see them. We made the evil ones friends to those who do not believe.

28 And when they commit an indecency, they say: "We found our fathers doing so"; and "God commanded us thus"; Say: "Nay, God never commands what is shameful ; do you say of God what you do not know?"

(Signs) Spelled Out 41:9-12

9 Say: Is it that you deny Him Who created the earth in two Days? And do you join equals with Him? He is the Lord of the Universe.

10 He set on [the earth], mountains standing firm, high above it, and bestowed blessings on the earth, and measure therein its provisions in four Days, alike for the seekers.

11 An He turned to the heaven when it was a smoke ; and He said to it and to the earth: "Come together, willingly or unwillingly." They said: "We do come (together), in willing obedience."

12 So He completed them as seven firmaments in two Days, and He assigned to each heaven its duty and command. And We adorned the lower heaven with lights, and provided it with guard. Such is the Decree of the Almighty, the All-Knowing.

The Wind-Curved Sandhills 46:33

Do they not see that God, Who created the heavens and the earth, and never wearied with their creation, is able to give life to the dead? Yea, verily He is All-Powerful.

Qaf 50:38
We created the heavens and the earth and all that is between them in Six Days, and no weariness touched Us.

The Winnowing Winds 51:47-48
47 With power and skill did We construct the Firmament and We are expanding it.
48 And We have spread out the (spacious) earth; How excellently We prepared it!

16. Life

The Windowing winds 51:56
I created the jinn and humankind only that they might worship Me.

Jonah 10:24
The likeness of the life of the present is as the rain which We send down from the skies; by its mingling arises the produce of the earth- which provides food for men and animals.
It grows till the earth is clad with its golden ornaments and is decked out in beauty; the people to whom it belongs think they have all powers of disposal over it ;
There reaches it Our command by night or by day, and We make it like a harvest clean-mown, as if it had not flourished only the day before! thus do We explain the Signs in detail for those who reflect.

The Cave 18:45-46
45 Set forth to them the similitude of the life of this world: It is like the rain which we send down from the skies; the earth's

vegetation absorbs it, but soon it becomes dry stubble, which the winds do scatter ; and God has power over everything.

46 Wealth and sons are allurements of the life of this world. But the things that endure, good deeds, are better in the sight of your Lord, as rewards, and better for hopes.

Iron 57:20

You should know, that the life of this world is but play and amusement, pomp and mutual boasting and multiplying, in rivalry among yourselves, in respect of money and children.

Here is a similitude: How rain and the growth which it brings forth, delight (the hearts of) the tillers; soon it withers; you will see it grow yellow; then it becomes dry and crumbles away.

But in the Hereafter is a severe retribution [for the devotees of wrong]. And Forgiveness from God and His Good Pleasure [for the devotees of God]. And what is the life of this world, but enjoyment of vanity.

Luqman 31:33-34

33 O mankind! Be mindful of your Lord, and fear a Day when no father can avail aught for his son, nor a son avail aught for his father. Verily, the promise of God is true; let not then this present life deceive you, nor let the chief deceiver deceive you about God. 34 Verily the knowledge of the Hour is with God [alone]. It is He Who sends down rain, and He Who knows what is in the wombs. Nor does any one know what he will earn on the morrow ; Nor does any one know in what land he is to die. Verily God is All-Knowing, All-Aware.

The Angels (The Initiator) 35:5

O men! Certainly the promise of God is true. Let not then this present life deceive you, nor let the chief deceiver deceive you about God.

The Cow 2:281
And fear the Day when you will be brought back to God. Then shall every soul be paid what it earned, and no one will be wronged.

The Romans 30:7
They know but the outer things in the life of this world, while they are heedless of the Hereafter.

The Story 29:77
"But seek, with the (wealth) which God has bestowed on you, the Home of the Hereafter, nor forget your portion in this world and do good to others, as God has been good to you, and seek not occasions for mischief in the land; for God loves not those who do mischief."

Consolation in difficult times

Solace, Consolation, Relief 94:5-6 :
So, verily, with hardship, there is ease:

Verily, with hardship there is ease.

Divorce 65:2-3, 7
And for those who fear God, He (ever) prepares a way out,
And He provides for him from sources he never expected. And if any one puts his trust in God, He will suffice him. For God will surely accomplish his purpose; verily, for all things has God appointed a due proportion.

7 God puts no burden on any person beyond what He has given him. After a difficulty, God will soon grant relief.

17. The resurrection and judgement day

The Troops 33:67-75

67 No just estimate have they made of God, such as is due to Him ; On the Day of Judgment the whole of the earth will be but His handful, and the heavens will be rolled up in His right hand ; Glory to Him! High is He above the Partners they attribute to Him!

68 The Trumpet will just be sounded, when all that are in the heavens and on earth will swoon, except such as it will please God [to exempt]. Then will a second one be sounded, when, behold, they will be standing and looking on!

69 And the Earth will shine with the Glory of its Lord, the Record [of Deeds] will be placed open; the prophets and the witnesses will be brought forward and a just decision pronounced between them; and they will not be wronged in the least.

70 And to every soul will be paid in full (the fruit) of its Deeds; and He knows best all that they do.

71 The deniers of the truth will be led to Hell in crowd; until, when they arrive, there, its gates will be opened. And its keepers will say, "Did not messengers come to you from among yourselves, rehearsing to you the Signs of your Lord, and warning you of the Meeting of This Day of yours?" The answer will be: "True; but the Decree of Punishment has been proved true against the deniers of the truth!"

72 (To them) will be said: "Enter ye the gates of Hell, to dwell therein ; and evil is this Abode of the Arrogants !"

73 And those who feared their Lord will be led to the Garden in crowds, until, behold, they arrive there; its gates will be opened; and its keepers will say: "Peace be upon you! well have you done! enter here, to dwell therein."

74 They will say: "Praise be to God, Who has truly fulfilled His

Promise to us, and has given us (this) land in heritage; We can dwell in the Garden as we will ; how excellent a reward for those who work (righteousness)!"

75 And you will see the angels surrounding the Throne on all sides, glorifying God with Praise to their Lord. And judgment shall be made between them in perfect justice, and it will be said: "Praise be to God, the Lord of the Worlds!"

The Prophets 21:103-104

103 (...) but the angels will meet them [with mutual greetings]: "This is your Day,- (the Day) that you were promised."

104 On that day, We will fold the heaven, like the folding of a book. As We initiated the first creation, so shall We reproduce it ; a promise We have undertaken, truly shall We fulfill it.

The Event 56:1-50

1 When the Event inevitable comes to pass,

2 There is no denying concerning its coming.

3 Bringing low [some]; exalting [others];

4 When the earth shall be shaken to its depths,

5 And the mountains shall be crumbled to atoms,

6 Becoming dust scattered abroad,

7 And you will be sorted out into three classes.

8 The Companions of the Right Hand;- What will be the Companions of the Right Hand?

9 And the Companions of the Left Hand,- what will be the Companions of the Left Hand?

10 And those Foremost [in Faith] will be Foremost [in the Hereafter].

11 These will be those Nearest to God,

12 In the Gardens of Bliss,

13 A number of people from those of first,

14 And a few from those of later times.

15 On Thrones encrusted (with gold and precious stones),

16 Reclining on them, facing each other.

17 Round about them will serve youths of perpetual freshness,

18 With goblets, shining beakers, and cups filled out of clear-flowing fountains,

19 Wherefrom they get no aching of the head nor any madness

20 And with fruits, any that they may select,

21 And the flesh of fowls, any that they may desire.

22 And Companions with beautiful, big, and lustrous eyes,

23 Like unto Pearls well-guarded.

24 A Reward for the deeds of their past life.

25 Not frivolity will they hear therein, nor any sinful talk

26 Only the saying, "Peace! Peace".

27 The Companions of the Right Hand,- what will be the Companions of the Right Hand?

28 [They will be] among lote trees without thorns,

29 Among Talh trees with fruits piled one above another,

30 In shade long-extended,

31 By water flowing constantly,

32 And fruit in abundance.

33 Neither limited, nor forbidden,

34 And on Thrones [of Dignity], raised high

35 We have created [their Companions] of special creation.

36 And made them virgin - pure ,

37 Beloved [by nature], equal in age,

38 For the Companions of the Right Hand.

39 Many from the first,

40 And many from those of later times.

41 The Companions of the Left Hand,- what will be the Companions of the Left Hand?

42 [They will be] in the midst of a Fierce Blast of Fire and in Boiling Water,

43 And in the shades of Black Smoke,

44 Nothing will be there to refresh, nor to please,

45 For that they were wont to be indulged, before that, in wealth and luxury,

46 And persisted obstinately in wickedness supreme!

47 And they used to say, "What! when we die and become dust

and bones, shall we then indeed be raised up again?-

48 "We and our fathers of old?"

49 Say: "Yea, those of old and those of later times,

50 "All will certainly be gathered together for the meeting appointed for a Day well-known.

The Reality 69:13-37

13 Then, when one blast is sounded on the Trumpet,

14 And the earth is moved, and its mountains, and they are crushed to powder at one stroke,-

15 On that Day shall the Great Event come to pass.

16 And the sky will be rent asunder, for it will that Day be flimsy,

17 And the angels will be on its sides, and eight will, that Day, bear the Throne of your Lord above them.

18 That Day you will be brought to Judgment ; not an act of yours that you hide will be hidden.

19 Then he that will be given his Record in his right hand will say: "Ah here! Read my Record!

20 "I did really understand that my Account would One Day reach me!"

21 And he will be in a life of Bliss,

22 In a Garden on high,

23 Its Fruits are within reach.

24 "Eat and drink, with full satisfaction; because of the good that you sent before you, in the days that are gone!"

25 And he that will be given his Record in his left hand, will say: "Ah! Would that my Record had not been given to me!

26 "And that I had never realized how my account (stood)!

27 "Ah! Would that [Death] had made an end of me!

28 " My wealth cannot avail me!

29 "My power has perished from me!"...

The Ascending Stairways 70:4-14

4 The angels and the spirit ascend unto him in a Day which duration is (as) fifty thousand years.

5 Therefore be patient with admirable patience.

6 They see the Day indeed as a far-off event.

7 But We see it quite near.

8 The Day that the sky will be like molten brass,

9 And the mountains will be like wool,

10 And no friend will ask after a friend,

11 Though they will be put in sight of each other,- the sinner's desire will be: Would that he could redeem himself from he Penalty of that Day by his children,

12 his wife and his brother,

13 his kindred who sheltered him,

14 And all, all that is on earth,- so it could deliver him

The Rising Of The Dead 75:6-14

6 He questions: "When is the Day of Resurrection?"

7 At length, when the sight is dazed,

8 And the moon is eclipsed.

9 And the sun and moon are joined together,-

10 That Day will Man say: "Where is the refuge?"

11 By no means! There is no refuge!

12 Before your Lord (alone), that Day will be the place of rest.

13 That Day will Man be told (all) that he put forward, and all that he put back.

14 Nay, man will be evidence against himself,

15 Even though he were to put up his excuses.

See also :

He Frowned! 80 :33-42

Those Who Drag Forth :34-46

The Calamity : 1-11

18. Some divine signs

(Signs) Spelled Out 41:39

And among His Signs in this: you see the earth barren and desolate; but when We send down rain to it, it is stirred to life and yields increase. Truly, He Who revived it can revive the dead. For He has power over everything.

The Romans 30:20-27, 46

20 Among His Signs in this, that He created you from dust; and then,- behold, you are men scattered far and wide !

21 And among His Signs is this, that He created for you mates from among yourselves, that you may dwell in tranquillity with them, and He has put love and mercy between your ; verily in that are Signs for people who reflect.

22 And among His Signs is the creation of the heavens and the earth, and the variations in your languages and your colours; verily in that are Signs for those who know.

23 And among His Signs is the sleep that you take by night and by day, and the quest that you make (for livelihood) out of His Bounty; verily in that are signs for people who listen.

24 And among His Signs, He shows you the lightning, for a fear and a hope, and He sends down rain from the sky and with it gives life to the earth after it is dead; verily in that are Signs for people who understand.

25 And among His Signs is this, that heaven and earth stand by His Command; then when He calls you, by a single call, from the earth, behold, you come forth.

26 To Him belongs every being that is in the heavens and on earth; all are devoutly obedient to Him.

27 It is He Who begins the process of creation; then repeats it; and for Him it is most easy. To Him belongs the loftiest similitude in the heavens and the earth ; for He is Exalted in Might, full of wisdom.

46 Among His Signs is this, that He sends the Winds, as heralds of Glad Tidings, giving you a taste of His Grace and Mercy,- that the ships may sail majestically by His Command and that you may seek of His Bounty, so that you may be grateful.

The Prophets 21:30-33

30 Do the disbelievers not see that the heavens and the earth were one of piece, and We opened them out ? And We made from water every living thing. Will they not believe?

31 And We have set on the earth mountains standing firm, lest it should shake with them, and We have made therein broad highways for them to pass through, that they may receive Guidance.

32 And We have made the heavens as a canopy well guarded, yet do they turn away from those Signs!

33 It is He Who created the Night and the Day, and the sun and the moon, each floating in its own orbit.

The Pilgrimage 22:5-7

5.O mankind! if you have a doubt about the Resurrection, (consider) that We created you out of dust, then from a small drop, then out of a leech-like clot, then out of a morsel of flesh, partly formed and partly unformed, so that We may make (it) clear for you ; and We cause whom We will to rest in the wombs for an appointed term, then do We bring you out as babes, then (foster you) that you may reach your age of full strength; and some of you are called to die, and some are sent back to the feeblest old age, so that they know nothing after having known (much), and (further). And you see the earth barren and lifeless, but when We pour down rain on it, it is stirred (to life), it swells, and it puts forth every kind of beautiful growth (in pairs).

6.This is so, because God is the Reality ; It is He Who gives life to the dead, and it is He Who has power over all things.

7.And verily the Hour will come, there can be no doubt about it, or about (the fact) that God will raise up all who are in the graves.

The Angels 35:27-28

27 See you not that God sends down rain from the sky? With it We then bring out produce of various colors. And in the mountains are tracts white and red, of various shades of color, and black intense in hue.

28 And so among men and crawling creatures and cattle, are they of various colors. Among His servants, those who are endowed with knowledge, stand in true awe of God. For God is Exalted in Might, Oft-Forgiving.

19. Muhammed and the Prophets

The Pen 68:1-6

1 Nun. By the Pen and the record which they (men) write,

2 You are not, by the Grace of your Lord, mad.

3 Verily for you is a Reward unfailing.

4 And you are of an exalted standard of character.

5 Soon wilt you see, and they will see,

6 Which of you is afflicted with madness.

The Prophets 21:51, 70-73, 75, 78, 83-91, 107

51 We bestowed aforetime on Abraham his rectitude of conduct, and well were We acquainted with him.

70 Then they sought a stratagem against him, but We made them the ones that lost most!

71 And We delivered him and Lut and directed them to the land

which We have blessed for the nations.

72 And We bestowed on him Isaac and, as an additional gift, Jacob, and We made righteous men of every one of them.

73 And We made them leaders, guiding by Our Command, and We inspired them to do good deeds, to establish regular prayers, and to practice charity; and they were devoted servants to Us.

74 And to Lut, too, We gave Judgement and Knowledge, and We saved him from the town which practiced abominations ; truly they were perverted people given to Evil.

75 And We admitted him to Our Mercy, for he was one of the Righteous.

76 And Noah, when he called aforetime ; We responded to him and delivered him and his family from great distress.

77 And We helped him against people who rejected Our Signs ; truly they were a people given to Evil; so We drowned them [in the Flood] all together.

78 And remember David and Solomon, when they gave judgement in the matter of the field into which the sheep of certain people had strayed by night ; We did witness their judgement.

83 And Job, when He cried to his Lord, "Truly distress has seized me, but You art the Most Merciful of those that are merciful."

84 So We responded to him, and We removed the distress that was on him, and We restored his family to him, and doubled their like,- as a Grace from Ourselves, and remembrance for worshipers.

85 And Ismael, Idriss [Enoch], and Zul-kifl [Ezekiel], all were of the patient ones ;

86 We admitted them to Our mercy; for they were of the

righteous ones.

87 And remember Zun-nun [Jonah], when he departed in wrath ; he imagined that We had no power over him! But he cried through the depths of darkness, "There is no god but You, glory to You, I was indeed of the wrongdoers !"
88 So We responded to him, and delivered him from distress, and thus do We deliver the faithful.

89 And Zakariya, when he cried to his Lord: "O my Lord! leave me not without offspring, though You art the best of inheritors."
90 So We responded to him, and We granted him Yahya [John], and We cured his wife for him. They used to vie one with the other in good deeds and to call upon Us hoping and fearing and humble themselves before Us.
91 And She who guarded her chastity, We breathed into her of Our spirit, and We made her and her son a sign for all people.

107 And We have sent you (Muhammad) not, but as a Mercy for all mankind.

The Heights 7:157
"Those who follow the messenger, the gentile Prophet, whom they find mentioned in the Torah and the Gospel ; for he commands them what is just and forbids them what is evil; he allows them as lawful what is good and pure and prohibits them from what is bad and impure; and he releases them from their heavy burdens and from the yokes that are upon them. So, those who believe in him, honour him, support him, and follow the light which is sent down with him,- These are the successful.

Women 4:63-166
163 We have have revealed to you, as We revealed to Noah and the Messengers after him ; We revealed to Abraham, Ismael, Isaac, Jacob and the Tribes, to Jesus, Job, Jonah, Aaron, and

Solomon, and to David We gave the Psalms.

164 Of some messengers We have already told you about ; of others We have not;- and to Moses God spoke directly.

165 Messengers delivering good news as well as warning, so that people will have no plea before God after the coming of the messengers. For God was ever Exalted in Power, Most Wise.

166 But God bears witness to what He has sent unto you. He has sent it with His own knowledge, and the angels bear witness. But God is sufficient as a witness.

Jonah 10:2

Is it a matter of wonderment to men that We have sent Our inspiration to a man from among themselves : "Warn mankind and give the good news to the Believers that they have before their Lord the lofty rank of truth." But those who deny the truth say: "This is indeed an evident sorcerer!"

20. The Quran

The Cow 2:1-5, 23-24

A.L.M. This is the Book in which there is no doubt, a guidance for those who are mindful of God;

Who believe in the Unseen, are steadfast in prayer, and spend out of what We have provided for them;

And who believe in the Revelation sent to you, and sent before your time, and are certain of the Hereafter.

They are on true guidance from their Lord, and these will be the successful.

23 And if you are in doubt as to what We have revealed to Our servant, then produce a Sura like thereunto; and call your witnesses or helpers besides God if your are truthful.

The Family of Imran 3:7

He it is Who has sent down to you the Book; In it are verses of established meaning ; they are the foundation of the Book ; others are allegorical. But those in whose hearts is perversity follow the part thereof that is allegorical, seeking discord, and searching for its hidden meanings, but no one knows its hidden meanings except God. And those who are firmly grounded in knowledge say: "We believe in the Book; the whole of it is from our Lord:" and none will grasp the Message except men of understanding.

The Event 56:75-80

75 I swear by the positions of the stars.
76 And that is indeed a mighty adjuration if you only knew,
77 That this is indeed a Qur'an Most Honourable,
78 In Book well-guarded,
79 Which none shall touch but those who are clean
80 A Revelation from the Lord of the Worlds.

The Family of Imran 3:1-3

A.L.M
God! There is no god but He,-the Living, the Self-Subsisting, Eternal.
It is He Who sent down to you, in truth, the Book, confirming what went before it; and He sent down the Torah [Law of Moses] and the Gospel [of Jesus] before this, as a guide to mankind, and He sent down the criterion [of judgement between right and wrong].

Al-Hijr Stoneland, Rock City 15:9

Verily it is We who have, sent down the reminder ; and We will assuredly guard it.

Made in the USA
Monee, IL
12 April 2024